GH00341370

SOUTH WEST WAY

A WALKER'S GUIDE TO THE COAST PATH

BOOK 1

THE NORTH COAST MINEHEAD TO PENZANCE

Castle Rock from North Walk

SOUTH WEST WAY
A WALKER'S GUIDE TO THE COAST PATH

BOOK 1
THE NORTH COAST MINEHEAD TO PENZANCE

Martin Collins

CICERONE PRESS
MILNTHORPE, CUMBRIA

ISBN 1 85284 025 0

For Diana and Paul who were with me constantly, in spirit if not in person, throughout the preparation of this guidebook.

All maps and photographs by the author

Front cover: St.Michael's Mount
Back cover: Trewavas Head

Contents

PREFACE

Around the middle of the last century, coastal walking was starting to gain popularity but had not yet suffered the kind of access problems which were to blight the history of rambling in this country. Sir Leslie Stephen, an accomplished mountaineer and walker of the period, wrote about the south-west coast in his essay *In Praise of Walking*,

> '...When you have made an early start, followed the coastguard track on the slopes above the cliffs, struggled through the gold and purple carpeting of gorse and heather on the moors, dipped down into quaint little coves with a primitive fishing village, followed by the blinding whiteness of the sands round a lonely bay, and at last emerged upon a headland where you can settle into a nook of the rocks, look down upon the glorious blue of the Atlantic waves breaking into foam on the granite, and see the distant sea-levels glimmering away until they blend imperceptably into cloudland; then you can consume your modest sandwiches, light your pipe, and feel more virtuous and thoroughly at peace with the universe than it is easy even to conceive yourself elsewhere...'

How times have changed! Following a journey by train and on foot around the British coast, Paul Theroux in his book *Kingdom by the Sea* writes,

> '...the nuclear power stations and the junkyards and the shallys and sewage farms: you could do anything you liked on the British coast, beside the uncomplaining sea. The seaside belonged to everyone.'

His may be a sweeping and jaundiced view from which the south-west peninsula could claim exemption, yet it points up a national disregard for our coastal margins which could once be relied upon to cleanse man's poisons at each tidal surge.

Pollution by oil, coal waste, sewage, toxic heavy metals, radioactive emissions and agricultural run-off threatens not just the shoreline of Britain and other parts of Europe but the health of offshore waters too. As new incidents of cynical or accidental dumping come to light, misuse of the sea reaches scandalous proportions. Fishing techniques incorporating new technology are achieving catches beyond the dreams of traditional fishermen and in the process have upset for ever the balance between harvesting and regeneration.

Our coastal lands fare little better. Saltmarsh is 'reclaimed' for agriculture or building development, industrial plants smother the environment with fumes and dust, sand-dunes and fragile foreshores suffer degredation from plastic jetsam and overuse, while greater personal mobility increases pressure for ever more car parks, holiday camps and amenities.

The outlook can appear hopelessly bleak unless account is taken of the many agencies working in the opposite direction to exploitation. Prominent among them are the Nature Conservancy Council, the National Trust, the Countryside Commission, Greenpeace, Friends of the Earth, the Marine Conservation Society, the Royal Society for the Protection of Birds and numerous practical conservation groups. Their collective mission is helped by the establishment of Nature Reserves, Areas of Outstanding Natural Beauty and of course National Parks, bringing to the public's attention the need for positive action to protect vulnerable habitats.

For the most part, the south-west peninsula has been spared the worst examples of coastal and offshore pollution. Its stunningly beautiful coastline is a national asset of inestimable value - more scenically varied and richly endowed than almost anywhere else in Europe. Nature has healed the scars of 19th century mining and quarrying to a large degree, while the depopulation of once vigorous coastal communities, replaced by holiday and retirement homes, has tended to create stronger links between the coast and recreation than ever existed before. Water sports, sea-cliff climbing and walking all enjoy immense popularity alongside less demanding holiday pursuits which people of all ages and dispositions enjoy.

The National Trust continues to guard large tracts of our Heritage Coast against present and future abuse and the walker will encounter at first hand the Trust's good work in providing access and waymarking. Indeed it is the interested walker who best obtains an overview of our coastline's delights. Casual strollers will turn back half a mile from the nearest car park, few bothering to explore the cliffs and coves, valleys and beaches separating them from the next resort. Such secrets are the reward for a little enterprise! Only those who set out equipped to face the elements and a modicum of leg-work will discover the essential character of this primordial frontier where land meets ocean.

Whether your coastal journey is a modest jaunt or a long distance trek, you will surely gain new perspectives, a sharpening of the senses and a fuller appreciation of the interplay between nature and the hand of man.

WHY A GUIDEBOOK?

Announcing to a friend that I was preparing a guide to Britain's south-west peninsula coast path provoked a flippant response. 'Surely', he quipped, 'by simply keeping the sea to one side you wouldn't need a guide at all!'

He was correct in the narrow sense that it would be possible to walk 'blind' and to muddle through without going wildly astray. But enjoyable walking, however modest or ambitious its range, is not about muddling through or taking lines of least resistance and missing many worthwhile stretches of path in the process.

Like my friend, the uninitiated may be forgiven for imagining that a coast path simply follows the sea's edge. If it were so, a guidebook would indeed lose much of its *raison d'être*, but the reality is very far removed from this simplistic notion. There are many reasons why coastal walking creates demands for a guidebook. The picture is complex when viewed in terms of the south-west peninsula as a whole, not only because there are often more ways than one of getting from A to B, but because those ways themselves are subject to change.

The relentless, destructive force of waves breaking against the margin of land, exacerbated by the effects of rain and gales, produces a unique erosion problem for coast paths. Where cliffs of soft rock are undermined, the path line is brought closer and closer to the edge until it finally slips into the sea. Here and there, subsidence on a grand scale has completely redrawn coastal topography, but for the most part it is a lurking threat to farmland, sheep, cattle and property - a threat which the coastal walker ignores at his peril. A comparable loss of footpath metres per year, with all the associated re-routing and waymarking, never occurs on inland routes, however well walked.

New building development, changes in land use, military ranges and camps all constitute obstacles to progress necessitating detours or periodic re-routing of coast paths. River crossings and some stretches of beach walking require advance knowledge of tides, wading points and the location of footbridges or ferries.

Undertaken along the interface between land and ocean, coastal walking provides a level of interest unsurpassed by any other kind of pedestrian travel. Not only will you encounter rich and varied flora, seabird populations, marine life and a fascinating range of geological features, but the hand of man is also well represented. From Iron Age promontory fortifications to satellite tracking stations, from the relics of 19th century mining and quarrying to the latest automatic

An acorn signpost

lighthouses, from old fishing harbours to busy holiday resorts, man's industry punctuates the long unfolding passages of cliff and foreshore. It is to this wealth of detail, not just to route directions, that the guidebook author addresses himself.

Clear and consistent waymarking would help unravel the coast path's complexities, but standards vary from excellent to non-existent. On reflection, this is hardly surprising. Quite apart from changes - official and unofficial - which occur from time to time, signs and posts are subject to being installed wrongly (or worse still not at all), to vandalism, to becoming misaligned and to concealment in undergrowth. Furthermore, a sea mist or low cloud and driving rain will disorientate the coastal walker as effectively as the hill walker and the consequences of a wrong turn in the vicinity of dangrous ground are no different. Unfortunately, the path line on OS maps is often out of date owing to the rapidity with which changes take place.

I therefore make no apologies for providing detailed route notes, even if in fine conditions they appear to be stating the obvious. In poor visibility or adverse weather (contrary to tourist brochures, the south-west coast is not always bathed in sunshine!), knowing where you are and where to aim for can save endless frustration casting about for the correct path.

Even though fragments of information here and there may have already been overtaken by events at the time of going to press, routing changes are likely to be minor ones and should not affect the relevance of background material in the text. For the latest footpath update, buy a copy of the South West Way Association handbook, published each year. It is obtainable from bookshops in the south-west region, or through membership of the Association, which does sterling work in improving the coast path. To join, send name, address and £4 (couples £5) to: Mrs. M.Mcleod, Membership Secretary, South West Way Association, 1 Orchard Drive, Kingskerswell, Newton Abbot, Devon TQ12 5DG.

Prompted by the SWWA, the Countryside Commission and local authorities continue to negotiate a truly coastal footpath round our south-west peninsula. Intransigent landowners, industrial interests, bureaucratic apathy and the vagaries of erosion all conspire against the realisation of this ideal but, piece by piece and year by year, improvements are made. Meanwhile, good reader, I trust you will benefit a little from having your appetite whetted, your curiosity roused and your hiking made more enjoyable by the contents of this literary 'companion'.

MARTIN COLLINS
November 1988

KEY TO MAPS

O	HAMLET, VILLAGE or TOWN CENTRE
⌐•⌐•⌐•	MAIN COASTAL PATH
••••••••	VARIANT
≈≈	PUBLIC ROAD
⌐⌐⌐	TRACK or FOOTPATH
▭ ▪	BUILDING; RUIN
≈	STREAM or RIVER
✚	INTERESTING CHURCH
⌂ ▲	LIGHTHOUSE; NOTABLE CLIFF or HILLTOP
+++++	RAILWAY LINE
⚠	YOUTH HOSTEL

ORIGINS AND DEVELOPMENT OF COASTAL PATHS

No doubt a few stretches of our coastal footpaths date back thousands of years. Mesolithic man, who foraged for shellfish and collected flints from pebble beaches to fashion arrowheads for hunting, would have worn the first narrow trods - some widened by centuries of use, many lost to the relentless march of erosion, buried by the plough or obliterated beneath building development.

Far more paths owe their existence to fishing and the need for communities to launch and beach their craft in various states of tides and weather, as well as gaining access to coves, headlands and neighbouring villages. Even so, long expanses of cliff and strand would rarely have seen a human visitor. Certainly there was no concept of 'holidaymaking' until the 19th century when an expanding railway network heralded the era of mass tourism for an increasingly industrial society. Until then, life for the common man on land adjacent to the coast would have been subject to the vagaries of climate and to the rigours of fishing or agriculture. Little time, energy or inclination would have remained to undertake travel for its own sake.

Later, more tracks and pathways would evolve in certain areas as coastal industries such as mining and quarrying began to flourish. The construction of harbours not only facilitated the import-export of industrial materials but also encouraged trade in commodities of all kinds. Before the advent of railway transport, ports large and small played vital roles in the nation's economy.

We can assume that more and more shoreline became familiar to these coastal inhabitants as they fished, laid nets, gathered seafood, plants and herbs, followed ships in distress and searched for survivors or valuable wreckage - in addition to the to-ing and fro-ing of everyday life.

However, by far the most significant factor in the evolution of our present coastal footpaths took place early in the 18th century, when the government of the day imposed heavy customs duties on imported luxury goods - especially wines and spirits - in order to generate much needed revenue. Fishing communities, quick to seize an opportunity to raise their living above subsistence level, turned to smuggling. Using their intimate knowledge of sea and coastline, fishermen and their fellow conspirators inland openly flaunted the law and created a thriving 'black economy', particularly along the south coast of

England. Indeed, even by 1724, Daniel Defoe had been moved to declare, '...that smuggling and roguing...is the reigning commerce of all this part of the English coast, from the mouth of the Thames to Land's End.

So seriously did it come to regard this lawlessness that in 1736 Parliament introduced an Act laying down severe penalties, including whipping and hard labour, for anyone found within 5 miles of the sea who could not satisfy the authorities that they had good reason to be there. The Act remained in force for almost a century and, of course, deterred any significant development of coastal walking and exploration for pleasure during that time.

Owing to elevated levels of duty, profits to be made from smuggling were considerable and it became widespread and highly organised, especially in the south-east where continental Europe is closest. No responsible government could tolerate this state of affairs indefinitely. Around 1815, a nightly shore patrol of the Kent and Sussex coast by sailors was set up. This was soon followed by the inauguration of the Coastguard Service in 1822, whereafter the entire coastline of the British Isles was regularly patrolled and coastal footpaths as we know them today became established.

Nearest the French coast, coastguards were stationed at 100 yard intervals (an astonishingly heavy deployment), while farther west and north each officer would cover from ½ to 3 or 4 miles. Coastguards were universally unpopular people, seen by the local communities as denying them access to a little luxury in otherwise extremely hard times. Not surprisingly, villagers refused to lodge officers in their houses, so specially designed stations were constructed with an eye to protecting their occupants from a hostile populace.

Conditions of service were rigorous. Duty hours, mostly at night, were long, to be worked in all weathers, over hazardous terrain and always carrying the added risk of encountering a determined band of smugglers. Coastguards were armed and initially there were some violent confrontations, resulting in injury and death on both sides; eventually, however, the rule of law prevailed and smuggling dwindled to a small-scale operation.

By the mid-1850's, the government's conversion to the principles of free trade had brought about dramatic reductions in tariffs and associated duties, so that contraband was no longer as profitable as it had once been and coastguard manning levels were reduced accordingly. Over the ensuing years, the Coastguard Service has shifted its attention to safeguarding the passage of shipping and co-ordinating rescue for those in difficulty on the coast itself or offshore.

Sadly, many lookout posts are now abandoned, boarded up or at the mercy of the elements. Footpaths, however, are far more durable in the long term and it is largely thanks to those early coastguard patrols that we have a South West Way today.

A BRIEF HISTORY OF THE SOUTH WEST WAY

The first dispute concerning access to the coast took place at Exeter Assizes as far back as 1838, when smuggling was still rife. John Ames, described as 'a gentleman of large fortune' had erected a wall around his recently acquired estate west of Lyme Regis, blocking off the coast path which had been in common use by locals for decades, if not centuries. All attempts at persuasion failed, so the local people took Ames to court - and won their case.

The outcome of such disputes were not always to be as happy as this however, although until the middle of the 19th century coastal walking would have been virtually hindrance-free, providing one had a convincing line to offer the coastguard! But as seaside resorts sprouted and improving transport began to feed visitors in increasing numbers to coastal locations, problems arose with inappropriate behaviour and abuse of the environment: in those days there was no country code!

So, uneducated in the need for a responsible attitude towards natural habitats, some visitors made nuisances of themselves and antagonised landowners. Measures were taken along the North Devon coast - notably at Clovelly, Lynton and Ilfracombe - to restrict public access to the cliffs by imposing admission tolls, erecting gates and fences or even closing off sections altogether. As can be imagined, such actions triggered considerable controversy, bringing into sharp focus the whole debate on recreational rights of way.

All our Long Distance Footpaths have had to be negotiated, piece by piece, with sometimes obstinate landowners; the South West Way, still technically incomplete as a continuous coastal footpath, is no exception.

By the beginning of this century, judges presiding over access disputes were still ruling in favour of landowners and against rights of way for purposes of pleasure or intellectual interest, however ancient the usage of such paths. Walking organisations were in their infancy and no match for their wealthy adversaries, whether landowning gentry or the new breed of property developers cashing in on the growth of seaside resorts. In 1932 the Rights of Way Act helped clarify the situation, while the Access to Mountains Bill of 1939 raised genuine hopes that mountain, moor, heath, cliff and downland would become more widely available to the general public. Ministerial interpretation of the access clauses and a tightening of the trespass laws, however, slammed the door in the face of the access movement and no improvements materialised.

First official interest in the notion of a South West Way came in a report by a government committee in 1941 under Lord Chief Justice Scott, set up to look at problems of rural land use and the establishment of National Parks. It was not until 1947, however, that a Town and Country Planning Act specifically froze development on the coast with no obligation to pay compensation. In the same year a government report specifically recommended the making of a coast path around the south-west peninsula, noting that over ⅓ of the Cornish coast was not open to the walker and that a total of almost 100 miles of extra footpath would be necessary to create a continuous route.

The appearance of the National Parks Commission (now the Countryside Commission) in 1949 did not produce instant progress, but eventually a South West Coastal Path was plotted out. Unfortunately, the Commission failed to use its teeth, taking the line of least resistance when confronted by an obstructive landowner - to the great detriment of the path which was routed unnecessarily and unsatisfactorily inland at such locations. More happily, the National Trust inaugurated its Enterprise Neptune project in May 1965 and has been acquiring sections of coastline for the nation's heritage ever since. The official opening of the Cornwall coast path took place in May 1973 at Newquay, and of the 'complete' South West Way (still technically unfinished) 5 years later. Many stretches remain which stray from the coast for one reason or another, despite the recommendations of 4 government reports. Each year some progress is made towards achieving the ultimate objective of a continuous and genuinely coastal footpath - a mile of new path here, a re-routing there or the removal of obstructions.

The South West Way Association

The Association was formed in the early 1970's when the idea of a long-distance footpath round the south-west coast was being implemented; those involved believed that little was being done on the South West Way which, in their opinion, was potentially a very fine footpath indeed. The objects of the Association are to secure the protection and preservation of an acceptable south-west coastal path and public access to that path. They provide a forum in which different interests connected with the path and its use can discuss problems of mutual concern.

They continually prod the authorities to complete the path and to see that it is properly waymarked and maintained, and are in constant communication with the Countryside Commission, the National Trust, the Exmoor National Park Authority and the four County Councils - Somerset, Devon, Cornwall and Dorset.

The Association disseminates information on the coast path to members of the public and produces an annual handbook which is sent free to members. This contains details of accommodation, a book list, rail and bus services, ferries and tide tables, as well as an update on the state of the path which undergoes minor changes from year to year.

Requests for membership should be sent to Mrs. M.McLeod, 1 Orchard Drive, Kingkerswell, Newton Abbot, Devon TQ12 5DG; tel (08047) 3061. Or to the Secretary - Mr. E.Wallis, 'Windlestraw', Penquit, Ermington, Nr. Ivybridge, Devon; tel (0752) 896237.

ABOUT THE NORTH COAST

The South West Way comprises many footpath segments linked together into a virtually continuous right of way. It stretches some 567 miles (912km) from Minehead in north Somerset to South Haven Point near Poole in Dorset and incorporates the Somerset and North Devon, North Cornwall, South Cornwall, South Devon and Dorset coast paths.

Although some sections of path are autonomous, with their own individual characteristics, a long-distance walker tackling stages of several days' or weeks' duration will tread the entire gamut of underfoot conditions reflecting an enormous variety of geographical features and terrain. High clifftop, sand and pebbly beaches, dismantled railway, woodland, estuary shore, grassy hillside, sand dunes, riverbank, country lane, farm track and urban pavement all bear the generic title 'coast path'.

A facet of coastal walking in the south-west absent from much (though not all) of Britain's hill country concerns the relative proximity of road, farmstead or settlement. Indeed, some stretches of path, more especially on the south coast, are little more than contiguous urban seafront owing to the density of resort development in sheltered locations such as Torbay.

There is no real contradiction, however, in stating that a great deal

Grass snake on the path

of coastal walking is wild and remote. Between villages or resorts, access inland may not exist, sometimes for many miles. Only in emergency would the crossing of hedges, walls, steep or impenetrable undergrowth etc. be justified to obtain help. You are travelling in a largely unusable corridor between sea and terra firma, barely beyond the waves and spray of high tides - an unstable mini-wilderness where the ocean's awesome and hypnotic presence is keenly felt.

Except in sparsely populated areas, farms and villages just inland sometimes offer hospitality of one kind or another - cream teas, camping, the occasional pub or bed and breakfast - but are reached only by time consuming detours. A fairly regular succession of amenities actually on the coast allows you to plan a day's hike around halts for meals and drinks, but the intervening miles do need the same careful consideration as their hill-country equivalents with regard to weather, distances, fitness, daylight hours etc.

Substantial parts of the coast path run along the perimeter of farm-land - often rough pasture or cultivated fields - but the nature of walking on that perimeter depends upon underlying geology, steep-ness and accessibility, and exposure to prevailing weather. In places you are held tightly between field fence and cliff edge, elsewhere you will be traversing rugged hillsides through gorse and thorn bushes or dense woodland.

By high summer, undergrowth on sheltered sections threatens to overwhelm the path. A thin scattering of local council employees, often with individual responsibility for many miles of footpath, use petrol-driven 'strimmers' to keep the way open, turning their hand to repairing stiles, gates and fences during the winter.

Gradients can be very steep, but with a few exceptions are less sustained than in mountain country. There are, however, more ups and downs per mile on average as the path dips to cove or beach before rising to the next clifftop. Owing to this frequency of ascent and descent, coastal walking is no 'easy option' and even hardened hill walkers can be surprised by the demands it makes on energy and overall fitness. Some sections are exceptionally easy on the legs and lungs, while others will challenge the fittest, but most fall into an intermediate category which leaves the walker comfortable enough to enjoy his surroundings.

Waymarking and path maintenance are carried out by local author-ities (except in the Exmoor National Park), who receive full grant aid from central government and thus incur no charge on local communities for this work. Unfortunately not all authorities honour their obligations and while standards are perceptibly improving in line with increasing public interest in coast path walking, omissions and neglect can be expected here and there. In general, the situation seems best adjacent to popular tourist areas where casual walking is undertaken by holidaymakers who expect paths to be clear and well signed (this does not include urban shoreline where a coast path, as such, is often non-existent). On wilder and remote parts of the coastline, conditions and waymarking can be less than satisfactory, though only the more experienced and resourceful walker is likely to reach there in the first place. Wherever the path crosses National Trust property, waymarking and standards of maintenance are usually impeccable.

A final word of warning about erosion and subsidence. I was lucky to escape with my life while researching for this book when the cliff edge at Cleave, near Crackington Haven on the north coast of Cornwall, disappeared in front of my feet, taking several metres of path with it. Two walkers ahead, approaching from the opposite direction, had seen the slippage starting and kept well back. My companion and I had no way of knowing the path was about to collapse and had we been there 5 seconds earlier would have been swept down to our certain deaths. I mention this incident not to scaremonger but to underline the need for vigilance, particularly after periods of very wet or windy weather.

The old coastguard paths have survived for well over a century, but it is a measure of the sea's power that man is in constant retreat. Softer rocks and shales are first to succumb and the walker is advised to take note of local geology; the granites and serpentine of the far south-west are more resistant to erosion. Watch carefully for overhangs, cracks and hollows and be extra cautious wherever the path runs close to the edge.

Red lifebelts and rescue kits - even emergency telephones - are installed at obviously hazardous locations. These are useful in certain situations (eg. rock-climbing accidents, getting into difficulties swimming or being cut off by the tide), but the kind of risks which threaten walkers are much more universal and cannot be safeguarded against except by attitude of mind and taking sensible precautions. In the event of an accident, contact the police who will, in turn, inform HM Coastguard and the relevant emergency services.

Finally, when best to go? May and June are favoured months in an average year, characterised by prolific wild flowers, freedom from undergrowth, long hours of daylight, usually good weather and an absence of holiday crowds. However, September and October can be equally fine. During both spring and autumn there is less pressure on accommodation, access to the coast and parking space, as well as on other amenities.

Path-side sea pinks

PUBLIC TRANSPORT

British Rail's main inter-city line from London, the Midlands and the North runs through Taunton, Exeter and Plymouth to Penzance, its southern terminus. Trains are frequent, fast and some provide sleeping car accommodation, but reservations for all seats are necessary on busy summer weekends. The following notes will indicate how to reach the coast path from railway stations, but more detailed enquiries will be needed to ascertain exact connections. Some branch lines operate in the summer months only.

Coast Path at	BR Station
MINEHEAD	Taunton, then Western National bus

BARNSTAPLE	Change at Exeter. Onward buses if required to Braunton, Ifracombe or Westward Ho!
BUDE	Exeter, then Jennings bus
PADSTOW	Bodmin Parkway, then bus (also to Polzeath)
NEWQUAY	Change at Par
HAYLE	Main line station (not all trains stop)
ST. IVES	Change at St. Erth
PENZANCE	Main line terminus

As an often less expensive long-distance alternative, National Express coaches operate from cities and towns all over the country to the south-west, for connection with local buses. For details contact your local National Express office or travel agent.

Bus travel in the south-west, as elsewhere in Britain, has undergone major transformation since deregulation. Some services have improved but in other areas remain patchy or non-existent. For the occasional bus ride, call at or phone the nearest Tourist Information Office (see 'Useful Addresses'); if, however, you require timetables for planning, consult the South West Way Association's annual booklet which lists bus operators, or write to the addresses below. Western National at Tower Street, Taunton, Somerset (for north Somerset), or at National House, Queen Street, Exeter EX4 3TF (for north Devon).

A book containing timetables for all public transport in Cornwall (bus, coach, rail, ferries and air) is available from Cornwall County Council, County Hall, Truro, tel: (0872) 74282 (weekdays).

Many more points on the coast path can be reached by using combinations of train, coach and bus. It is worth bearing in mind that winter services are less frequent and may need to be augmented by taxi, private car or even hitching if access to or from remote locations is sought.

ACCOMMODATION - CAMPING, YOUTH HOSTELS, BED AND BREAKFAST

This chapter will be of greater interest to long-distance walkers who need to plan ahead than to those undertaking day walks from a central base, although all coastal walkers will benefit from knowing what to expect along the way.

Approaches to travelling on foot vary from the backpacker who carries a lightweight tent and equipment and seeks out each night 'wild' pitches in lonely places, to the patroniser of luxury hotels and restaurants. Between these extreme ends of the spectrum lie the bed-and-breakfaster, the youth hosteller and those who combine various forms of accommodation according to circumstances.

Owing to the remote nature of much of the north coast, lightweight camping is a real option and gives the backpacking walker maximum flexibility over where to end the day. However, camping is not without problems of its own. Campsites *per se* are relatively thin on the ground, tend to open only in the summer and are not necessarily conducive to a restful night's sleep! (A list of campsites is issued to members of the Camping and Caravanning Club of Great Britain, 11 Grosvenor Place, London SW1W 0EY.)

Genuine backpackers able to cope with a minimum or complete absence of facilities can ask at farms adjacent to the coast (individuals or couples only - no large groups). Farmers are nearly always friendly and sympathetic, but **never** pitch on farmland without asking permission first. You will be able to obtain fresh water, possibly milk too, but once in the field you are shown to, you are on your own. Always offer to pay for the pitch, even if payment is sometimes refused: this maintains goodwill and smooths the way for future lightweight campers.

Finding true 'wild' pitches is possible for experienced backpackers who know what to look for. Much depends on wind strength and direction (actual and expected), for there is little shelter from an onshore blow. Most promising locations are stream valleys and the tops of beaches. Pure water is not easy to come by as streams often flow through farms and pasture on their way to the sea; springs, however, are usually clear and are marked on OS 1:25,000 maps. If in doubt, either use purifying tablets or be prepared to carry water from the last reliable source.

You will pass numerous wild pitches which are too close to habitations to use. Discretion and sensitivity to other path users are essential in choosing a pitch - remember that large sections of path run through designated Areas of Outstanding Natural Beauty or Heritage Coast. The National Trust does not allow camping on its land nor on its farms.

The backpacker's code of leaving no trace of an overnight pitch assumes extra significance on a coastal route where others will pass by after you. However, it is a style of travel which offers independence and close contact with the environment; furthermore, when combined with camping at farms and official sites, accommodation costs are reduced to their lowest level.

Apart from an inherent lack of home comforts such as hot baths and

Tintagel Youth Hostel (top right) on Dunderhole Point

clean sheets, camping's main disadvantage is the need to carry a heavier rucksack. This imposes additional strain on the feet and joints and turns hilly stages into altogether more strenuous propositions. The best advice is to keep rucksack weight as light as possible and to make one or two 'dry runs' near home to familiarise yourself with the backpacking process.

Youth hostels are situated at Minehead, Lynton, Ilfracombe, Instow, Hartland, Boscastle, Tintagel, Treyarnon Bay, Newquay, Perranporth, Hayle, Land's End and Penzance (for details see 'Useful Addresses'). Of course, these are too few for long-distance walkers to rely on exclusively but used in conjunction with bed and breakfast or camping, youth hostels provide cheap and convivial overnight halts. Individual hostels, often in marvellous settings, could be used as a base for 2 or 3 nights' stay, enabling expeditions to be made along the coast path in both directions.

For details of north coast hostels and application forms, write to the YHA Area Office, Belmont Place, Stoke, Plymouth; tel: (0752) 562753. Advance booking is necessary during the busy summer months, but it is worth remembering that there is no upper age limit for members and that motorised transport can be used. For membership, write to the YHA, St. Albans, Herts. AL1 2DY.

Bed and breakfast·establishments will be found in abundance at villages and towns along the coast path or a short distance off it. There are substantial sectors of path however, which are devoid of any human settlement and it is there that accommodation problems can arise. When arriving at a town with a Tourist Information Office, staff will happily assist in finding you a bed for the night, but if you require the security of advance bookings, more organised planning will have to be done. In their annual handbook, the South West Association publish a list of recommended bed and breakfast places, including phone numbers and prices; holiday accommodation books obtainable from newsagents will also yield helpful information.

In the author's experience it is quite unnecessary to reserve accommodation except during the school holiday period and perhaps a fortnight either side. If it is imperative to book a sequence of bed and breakfasts in advance, err on the side of underestimating daily mileage. Adverse weather, injury, fatigue or an unforeseen delay can interrupt the journey and set you on a gruelling treadmill from which it is hard to escape. Far better to keep in hand time and energy with which to enjoy each day's destination.

Most guest-house proprietors, innkeepers and hoteliers on or near the coast path will do what they can to dry out wet gear and satisfy healthy appetites. Many will provide packed lunches on request and walkers are assured of a comfortable night's rest away from the elements, though it is not always easy to make an early start.

OBTAINING SUPPLIES AND REFRESHMENTS

With the exception of a few stretches of remote and uninhabited coast, there is usually no difficulty in buying food along the path - even tiny hamlets often boast a Post Office/General Store. It is wise to carry rations for unexpected delays however, as well as extra energy food (fruit, chocolate etc.) to help you deal with more strenuous terrain. Only in two or three areas along the north coast are you more than a couple of hours' walk from a place of refreshment, whether it be pub, cafe, hotel, restaurant, kiosk or shop. At the season's height, some strength of will is required to resist the coffees, pub lunches, cream teas and ice-creams which seem to beckon on all sides!

It is vital to realise, however, that many such fleshpots are seasonal.

Seafront refreshments at Woolacombe

Walkers setting out in months other than May to September will encounter a vastly restricted choice. Indeed, long-distance winter expeditions present considerable logistical problems, even though generally milder weather in the south-west is more favourable for hiking than conditions in hill country further north.

Since only a small number of sizeable towns occur on or near the coast (namely Minehead, Lynmouth, Ilfracombe, Barnstaple, Bideford, Bude, Padstow, Newquay, Hayle, St. Ives and Penzance), walkers wishing to purchase unusual items urgently will be faced with a delay or a journey by public transport.

Banks are few and far between and minor branches often open only one or two days per week. Credit cards may be acceptable in larger guest-houses, hotels and restaurants, but payment for goods and services must otherwise be paid for by cash or cheque. It is certainly prudent to carry plenty of cash or use a Girobank account - Post Offices are more common and are open longer hours.

CLOTHING AND EQUIPMENT

For the majority of coastal walkers who set out during the months of longer daylight hours and warmer conditions from April to October, a balance has to be struck between hiking comfort and protection from the elements. Even in high summer it may be wet and windy at times

24

and can feel unseasonably chilly. Then shell clothing (preferably breathable) over a light shirt and shorts will often suffice while on the move, with a jumper and lightweight trousers to slip on when you stop. In early spring or autumn, a thicker shirt, extra sweater or pile jacket, woolly hat and breeches or windproof trousers may be needed.

Burning ultra-violet radiation from summer sunshine is accentuated on the coast by reflection off the sea and sand. Tempting though it may be to wear very little on such glorious days, you are just as vulnerable to sunburn as beachgoers. Shoulders, arm tops, foreheads, nose and fronts of legs can become painfully burned while the preoccupations of the route hold your attention: good advice is to avoid sleeveless garments, to wear a brimmed sunhat and light, loose clothing. Applying a high-factor suncream to exposed skin is a wise precaution, especially for fair skinned people or those unaccustomed to bright sunshine.

A heat wave may be the holidaymaker's dream but can produce gruelling conditions for walkers. When you are hot, thirsty and tired, sunshine becomes as much the enemy as cold is in winter. There is precious little shade along the coast path and although good for splashing over yourself, stream water is not usually safe to drink. Unless you know there are refreshment points on route, always carry some fresh water in hot weather.

Sunlight can be dazzling when walking westwards - a pair of polarizing sunglasses will relieve your eyes of strain and cut out specular reflections on the sea, allowing you to look through its surface as an added bonus.

Needless to say, carrying a change of clothes in the rucksack is essential if you are planning a walk of several days duration or longer. Clothing can get as damp from perspiration as from rain and with the physical effort of walking will soon need washing! Hikers using hostels or guest-houses may need to be more fastidious than campers who have only themselves for company and can afford to wait a day or two for their next shower! A swimming costume and towel will open up possibilities for bathing when the opportunity arises.

It is assumed that backpackers know what gear to take along so this will not be dealt with here. Any additional items to include can be ascertained from these introductory chapters. Camping Gaz, methylated spirit or paraffin wax for stoves are only obtainable in larger towns or well appointed campsites, as are water purifying tablets, photographic film and batteries and other articles of a specialised nature.

Rucksacks are important pieces of equipment, not just for the backpacker whose 'mobile home' they contain, but for the hosteller and bed-and-breakfaster too. Spare clothing, cagoule and overtrousers, food, water, first aid kit (including telephone coins, and emergency whistle), toilet gear, books, camera and film, maps, compass and guidebook will all sometimes need to be packed away, especially in wet weather when a number of plastic bags will ensure everything is kept dry. Add a torch for off-season hiking.

Rucksack weight above about 12lbs. (5kg) is carried more comfortably when a flexible lightweight frame or insert and a hip belt are built into the pack design. Such features spread the load, provide contour rigidity against the back and aid postural stability when climbing stiles or rocks, particularly in a wind. Straps allowing potentially wet and muddy items to be attached externally are useful. Even day walkers will need a robust, if smaller, pack for long or uninhabited stretches or for out-of-season hiking.

Binoculars or a monocular will bring a good deal of pleasure, not only from viewing along the coast but providing close-ups of seabirds, seals, shipping and inaccessible shoreline. If your camera will take filters, be sure to use a UV eliminator which doubles as protection from salt spray. A polarizer will add depth to colour shots and give you sometimes surprising glimpses of what lies underwater. A pocket-sized radio is useful for obtaining weather and shipping forecasts as well as for entertainment and news if backpacking, but as with all such non-essentials, personal preferences and accumulative pack weight will be the arbitrators.

Finally footwear - for a number of reasons not as straightforward a subject as one might imagine! The author has met long-distance back-packers who made do with trainers and has himself used them successfully at times. They have three main drawbacks however, which detract from their advantages of comfort, light weight and low cost.

First they offer no ankle support and this cannot be ignored as much of the going is rough, sometimes steep and often requires accurate foot placement. Carrying a heavy pack simply exacerbates the problem. Second, few trainers possess soles suitable for gripping on loose slopes. Although cleated rubber soles as fitted to boots also fail to provide traction on smooth, wet surfaces, trainers give little 'bite' in mud or wet grass either. Third, you will get wet feet very quickly - from rain certainly, but more commonly from moisture-laden grasses and undergrowth which in summer curl over the path, obscuring its surface and acting as a continuous footbath! In such conditions, it has to be said, leather boots too will become saturated although with help from gaiters or anklets the process is retarded.

In their favour, trainers are ideal for easy sections of path in dry weather and in accommodation or when eating out. Having once become wet, they do dry out faster than boots.

Heavy walking boots are generally considered unnecessary for any kind of rough walking unless cold and the wearing of crampons are likely factors. Probably the best footwear for the South West Way are lightweight leather boots with good tread depth, ankle support and well waxed for maximum water resistance. Two pairs of socks will help prevent blisters, but at the end of the day the only guarantee of foot comfort is previous mileage to harden feet and break in boots.

MAPS, TIDES AND RIVER CROSSINGS

This guidebook covers the north coast path and its variants in considerable detail but there remains a strong case for supplementing its use with Ordnance Survey maps. A compass weighs next to nothing and will rarely be needed, but the author has found one useful on a few occasions when a sudden sea mist rolled in or it was necessary to navigate off route on little used rights of way.

1:50,000 scale maps are perfectly adequate for walking on the south-west coast, though bear in mind that the path line may have changed here and there since the last revision or may not be marked at all. 1:25,000 scale maps show a wealth of detail and are especially valuable to those interested in archaeological or industrial remains: there are rather too many sheets involved for the longer-distance walker to carry.

1:50,000 Landranger maps required for the north coast are (in walk order):

No.	Title
181	Minehead and Brendon Hills
180	Barnstaple and Ilfracombe
190	Bude and Clovelly
200	Newquay and Bodmin
204	Truro and Falmouth
203	Land's End and The Lizard

1:25,000 Pathfinder maps (First or Second Series) available for the north coast are (in path order):

No.	Title
SS 84/94	Minehead
SS 64/74	Lynton

SS 44/54	Ilfracombe
SS 43/53	Barnstaple
SS 42/52	Bideford
SS 21/31	Kilkhampton
SS 20/30	Bude
SX 19	St. Gennys
SX 08/18	Tintagel
SW 87/97	Padstow and Wadebridge
SW 86/96	Newquay
SW 75	Perranporth
SW 54/64	Camborne (North)
SW 63	Camborne (South)
SW 33/43	St. Ives and Penzance (North)
SW 32/42	Land's End

The ebb flow of tides will rarely escape your notice while walking on the coast path. For the most part, this diurnal cycle is of incidental interest, determining whether or not the foreshore rocks and beaches are exposed and accessible. In at least two situations, however, tides assume greater significance for the coastal walker.

One of these is where the route or a desirable alternative takes to the beach: especially if this entails walking beneath high cliffs, there is a real danger of becoming cut off by a rising tide. Many such incidents involving unwary holidaymakers occur each year and although the outcome is usually a happy one, perhaps following rescue by rope or helicopter, fatalities do happen.

It goes without saying that to embark upon a lengthy beach walk without prior knowledge of escape routes or times of low and high water is asking for trouble. Raising the alarm is extremely difficult from the base of cliffs and lone walkers are at a further disadvantage if climbing to safety is the only option.

Freak waves of greater height than average occuring at unpredictable intervals are an added hazard to beware of when scrambling or walking close to the sea's edge. Lives are lost with depressing regularity, not always from conscious risk taking but through a lack of understanding of how the ocean behaves.

The other occasion when tide times become vital to the walker concerns the crossing of river mouths by wading or ferry. On the north coast, only the River Gannel at Newquay can be negotiated on foot but along the south coast, river crossings are more frequent (for details, see this guidebook's sister volume - *The South Coast - Penzance to Poole*).

Reference to route notes in this guidebook provides all the relevant information on ferries wherever they occur along the coast path. Some are seasonal, others only operate each side of high water, others still are year-round and run at regular intervals from early till late. Low water can affect the embarkation and landing points of ferries and one should always be prepared to adopt an alternative strategy if for one reason or another the ferry should not be running.

On some estuaries such as the River Taw between Braunton Burrows and Appledore and from Hayle Towans to Lelant, passenger ferries have fallen into disuse, regrettably involving the walker in considerable detours. Occasionally it is possible to find someone willing to take you across at such places in their own boat but even this depends on the tide and weather being favourable. Offering payment will encourage good relations between walkers and the boating fraternity!

Wading a river mouth is not always as simple as it sounds. After periods of rain and during the tide cycle except at low water, the channel may be too deep and the current too swift for safe human passage. In fact, footbridges are uncovered in the River Gannel at low water but the most downstream one is removed after the summer season and it is here that wading is possible (see 'Route Notes').

Recourse to tide tables rather than casual observation is recommended to establish times of high and low water, though potential delay to walkers on the north coast will be minimal compared to that on the south coast. Tide tables are available from many newsagents

The Rock to Padstow ferry across the River Camel

and bookshops in the south-west, while the South West Way Association publish figures for Newquay in their annual handbook (see 'Useful Addresses'). Tide times are also often displayed at seafronts and harbours.

WEATHER

Over a half of Cornwall is situated less than 5 miles (8km) from the sea and even central Devon locations are only some 18 miles (30km) distant. This proximity to vast expanses of open water on 3 sides differentiates the climate of the south-west peninsula from that of the rest of Britain. One effect is to reduce both seasonal and diurnal variations in temperature so that there is less fluctuation than further up the mainland. Along the north coast of Cornwall and Devon, the average mean temperature is 11 deg.C - a little lower towards the north-east of Devon and into Somerset.

June is usually the sunniest month, December the dullest and there is more winter daylight than anywhere else in Britain. In the extreme south-west, around 1,750 sunshine hours per year can be expected; taking the year as a whole, this is the country's warmest spot, along with the Isles of Scilly.

Sea temperatures are lowest in late February/early March and because they also influence the adjacent land, February is normally the area's coldest month, with average means of between 1.5 and 5 deg.C. The lowest recorded temperature was – 16.7 deg.C at Cullompton, Devon in January 1940.

July and August are the warmest months, with mean maxima of 19 to 21 deg.C (usually reached in mid-afternoon), though the relatively cold sea prevents the coast itself from becoming quite as warm as inland. The highest regional temperature in recent years - 33.9 deg.C - was recorded at Ellbridge in Cornwall during 1976, the 'Year of the Drought'.

Relative humidity - on average around 80% - is higher in winter and at night, though during heavy fog or persistent rain it can reach 100%. Rainfall for the region varies between 1,200mm (47in.) and 800m (31in.) per annum - November, December and January being wettest, April and June driest. Heavy downpours associated with thunderstorms can occur anytime but mainly over the land in summer and over a warmer sea in winter. The sea's presence produces a more uniform incidence of thunderstorms throughout the year than farther into the mainland where they occur principally during the summer.

Beaufort No.	Designation/average speed in knots	Effects of wind on the sea
0	Calm - under 1	Smooth, glassy sea.
1	Light - 2	Small, scale-like ripples without crests.
2	Light - 5	Small waves, still short and smooth but more pronounced.
3	Light - 8	White caps forming but still mostly smooth. Occasional white foam appearing.
4	Moderate - 13	Waves still small but longer. White caps fairly general.
5	Fresh - 18	Moderate-sized waves now long and more pronounced. White caps everywhere. Occasional spray forming.
6	Strong - 24	Formation of larger waves. Crests break and leave areas of white foam. Some spray.
7	Strong - 30	Sea heaps up. Long streaks of foam begin to form along the wind direction. More spray. (Some difficulty walking against the wind.)
8	Gale - 37	Large waves with very long crests. Spray blown off wave crests. Long, thick streaks of foam. (Walking progress considerably impeded.)
9	Severe gale - 44	Mountainous seas. Dense streaks of foam along direction of wind. Wave crests begin to topple and roll over. Spray may affect visibility.
10	Storm - 52	Towering, tumbling waves with long, overhanging crests. Sea white with foam. Visibility restricted by spray. (Considerable structural damage on land.)
11	Violent storm - 60	Extremely mountainous sea, white and foaming. Drastically reduced visibility. (Widespread damage on land.)
12	Hurricane - 68 +	Air filled with driving foam and spray as wave crests are torn off by the wind. Sea completely white and frothy. Visibility very difficult. (Devastating damage on land but rarely experienced.)

(Walkers should take care not to linger on high, open clifftops during thunderstorms owing to the chance of lightning strike.)

Snowfall is rarer here than elsewhere in Britain and usually falls on 10 or less days a year, while most coastal locations see a ground frost on between 35 and 60 days.

Sea (or 'advection') fog forms when moist, warm air is in contact with a relatively cold sea surface. It is most frequent in spring and early summer along the coast itself and immediately inland. At St. Mawgan near Newquay, there are around 50 days per year on average when visibility is less than 200 metres; months most affected by sea fogs in the south-west are June and July.

Because Atlantic depressions are more frequent in winter, winds then are usually strongest. As one would expect on such an exposed peninsula, south-westerly gales are more commonly experienced than in the rest of England. The extreme south-west of Cornwall can expect 25 or more gale days per year when mean wind speeds exceed 34 knots over any 10 minute period. Gale days decrease as you move inland and north-east. Extreme wind speeds occasionally occur, such as 103 knots recorded at Gwennap Head, near Land's End, on 15th January 1979 -not the sort of weather for a cliff path walk!

In fact, wind speed and direction is of particular concern to walkers as it can hinder progress on coast paths more seriously than any other single factor. Wind speed is assessed visually by the Beaufort Scale, an international standard for mariners which can be of considerable interest to coastal walkers, particularly in conjuction with broadcast shipping forecasts.

Weather forecasts are provided by national BBC radio and television, as well as by the press, and will provide general indications to the expected weather countrywide. However, as with all geographically unique regions, parts of the south-west peninsula often create local climates of their own, much to the chagrin of the tourist industry which stands to lose custom from adverse weather forecasts which tend to tar large areas with the same brush!

Forecasts on local radio and television are more reliable and the BBC Shipping Forecasts at 1.55pm. and 5.50pm. are especially useful if you are already familiar with meteorological terminology; sea area Lundy and Land's End Coastal Station are relevant to the north coast. Weather forecasts for the south-west may also be obtained by telephoning (0898) 600291; (0898) 500481; or (0898) 333598.

HOW TO USE THIS GUIDE

The tradition of walking the south-west coast path in an anti-clockwise direction springs from there being more miles in total with wind and weather behind you than against you. Expeditions on the north coast alone, however - rather less than half the path's overall distance of 567 miles - gain little from this tradition as the predominant direction of travel faces south-west. Nevertheless, waymarking tends to favour the anti-clockwise walker, who in any case will probably prefer a more north-easterly starting point for a long-distance trek in order to reduce initial journey time from other parts of the country. The picture is reversed of course for long-distance walkers starting the southern half of the route from Penzance! (For details see this guidebook's sister volume - *The South Coast: Penzance to Poole.*)

Attempting to describe the path in both directions at once would be unwieldy to say the least, so the author has adopted an anti-clockwise stance for all the route notes. It is normally a simple matter to reverse each section by reference to a map and by intelligent observation at path junctions and the like. With this book in your hand you are extremely unlikely to go astray!

Route notes are accurate when going to press and will take the guesswork out of tricky stretches of path while sketching in points of interest along the way. To assist forward planning of both day walks and continuous long-distance hikes, the coast path has been divided into 21 sections, each a day's walk in length and beginning and ending at places where there are amenities for refreshment or accommodation (or access inland to them). Three longer stages of roughly a week each are introduced by brief descriptions. These are suggestions only and may well be exceeded by strong walkers, or split into shorter increments if desired. For distances between places along the way, consult the mileage table at the back of this book.

Each section begins with a summary of its length, the kind of terrain and gradients to be expected, along with details of amenities and access points. An attempt has been made to grade the walking for difficulty, though such an exercise will always be subjective. 'Easy' means mostly flat going on good paths, tracks or urban pavements. 'Moderate' means average gradients of the kind encountered in gentle hill country, with well-defined paths of good surface. 'More difficult' denotes rough, awkward terrain or considerable ups and downs, unsuitable for very young, elderly or inexperienced walkers. 'Strenuous' means successive big ascents and descents on rugged paths, often steep and remote from roads or habitations.

In the text, places reached on the path are followed in brackets by the amenities they provide. 'All shops, services and accommodation' suggests the availability of most consumer goods, a range of places to eat and stay at, and the existence of banks, Post Office, telephones, toilets etc. A few other features such as Information Centres, museums, etc. are also mentioned but the lists cannot claim to be comprehensive in scope.

Alternative routings (variants) appear in smaller type, while notable places or features along the path are picked out in heavier type for quick identification.

Sketch maps accompanying the text are not intended to supplant the use of Ordnance Survey maps and will not help you re-establish your position if you become completely lost in a sea mist or low cloud and driving rain, or if you have strayed badly off route. However, used in conjunction with the detailed Route Notes, the sketch maps will steer you happily down the coast - for 99% of the time problem-free. Drawn to scale, they paint a broad picture of the walking ahead and what to look out for, enabling you to identify linear progress quickly and easily. (Please note that twists and turns round coastal indentations cannot be readily accommodated in the page layout, so always refer to direction north on each map to orientate it with compass or OS sheet.) With this book open in front of you, the sketch maps read from the bottom of the page to the top, corresponding with the coast unfolding ahead.

No individual or organisation can hope to monitor all changes which take place on the path through erosion, land-use alteration or obstructions. It would therefore be appreciated if walkers would note down any significant new cliff-falls or unofficial path diversions etc. on the blank pages provided at the end of this book. The South West Way Association would like to hear from you - please write giving details of your observations to Eric Wallis, 'Windlestraw', Penquit, Ermington, Nr. IVYBRIDGE, Devon PL21 0LU.

The book concludes with notes on tin and copper mining in Cornwall, a list of Useful Addresses, a Bibliography, a Coast Path Code, a Sea-bathing Code and a Distances Table.

Rounding Morte Point

SOUTH WEST WAY

Book 1
THE NORTH COAST

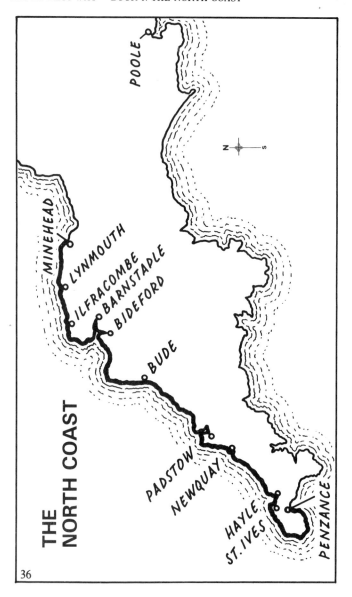

POOLE

N

S

MINEHEAD

LYNMOUTH

ILFRACOMBE

BARNSTAPLE

BIDEFORD

BUDE

THE
NORTH COAST

PADSTOW

NEWQUAY

HAYLE

ST. IVES

PENZANCE

CHAPTER 1
Minehead to Westward Ho!
(76 miles - 122km)

From the busy little resort of Minehead, the coast path climbs onto high moorland clifftops above the Bristol Channel, dropping back to sea level via picturesque Bossington. A long pebble bank leads on to Porlock Weir, whereafter you pass tiny Culbone Church up through luxuriant woods into the Glenthorne Estate. Far above the sea for several miles, the path emerges at Foreland Point and descends Countisbury Hill to the sister villages of Lynmouth and Lynton.

Curious land forms in Valley of the Rocks give way to woods and a marvellously elevated approach to Heddon's Mouth with its romantically sited inn. Eroded cliffs precede a brief moorland stretch followed by a stiff ascent to the Great Hangman, highest point on the entire South West Way and an exciting viewpoint. A descent to Combe Martin brings you out of the Exmoor National Park, on round a dramatic headland and over a hill to Ilfracombe.

Easy walking to Lee Bay grows more strenuous near Bull Point lighthouse but soon Morte Point is rounded and Woolacombe's great sandy beach takes you along to Putsborough and Baggy Point. In surfing country now, the path passes Croyde and Saunton, weaving through the remarkable dune system of Braunton Burrows to the mouth of the River Taw. Close to RAF Chivenor, a dismantled railway track connects Braunton with the bustling town of Barnstaple, where more railway track bed walking - a recently opened stretch of path - takes you to Instow and the ferry to Appledore. After having detoured right round the Taw estuary, the coast proper is regained at Westward Ho!

SECTION 1 - Minehead to Porlock Weir (or Porlock); 9 miles (14km)

A gradual ascent on well used paths to 1,000ft. high (300m) coastal moorland. A steep descent then level walking behind a pebble bank with an awkward stretch over large stones at the end.
B&B and seasonal refreshments at Bossington. Shops, services, accommodation and refreshments just off route at Porlock.   Grading - moderate.

Minehead - near the start of the path

MINEHEAD *(all shops, services and accommodation. Nearest BR station is Taunton, with connecting Western National bus service. On coach routes from London and Bristol. Youth hostel 1½ miles (2.5km) south. Early closing Wednesday.)*

Minehead, once comprising Higher Town, Lower Town (almost completely destroyed by fire in 1791) and Quay Town, dates back to at least the 12th century. In the early 1700's, the harbour would have been busy with the comings and goings of sailing vessels trading between here, Ireland and America. A thriving shipyard existed (where today's Inshore Lifeboat is stationed,) servicing the 40 or so ships based here, as well as visiting sloops and barques. Today all that remains is a little commercial fishing from the harbour, and seasonal pleasure craft. George Luttrell's jetty, built in 1616 and later extended, still stands, but a 700ft. (213m) iron promenade pier of more recent construction was demolished during the Second World War

For a time in the 19th century, Minehead enjoyed a limited boom as an up-market holiday resort; nowadays, the town remains a busy destination for holidaymakers of all kinds. The air is bracing, there is a fine stretch of pebble beach and a good range of shops and entertainments, including the 'Somerwest World' theme park. Rising as a conspicuous landmark on higher ground above the harbour is the 14th century tower of St. Michael's church.

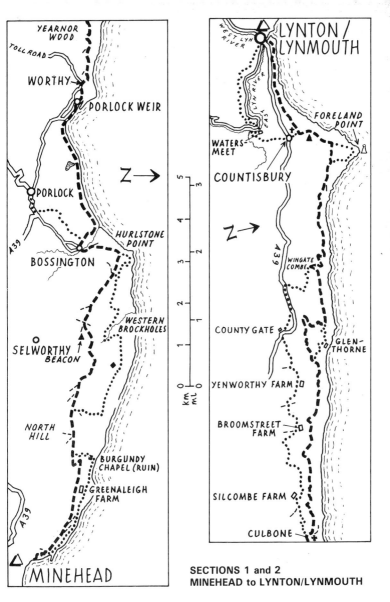

SECTIONS 1 and 2
MINEHEAD to LYNTON/LYNMOUTH

There are several alternatives linking Minehead with Bossington, the first village to be encountered. For simplicity's sake, the official coast path and one main variant are described below. The official routing takes a gradually ascending line onto wild, open moorland, staying well back from the steep convex slopes of these distinctive Exmoor cliffs, which drop their rounded shoulders into the Bristol Channel from tops near the 1,000ft. (300m) contour. If good linear progress is important, or you'd like a gentle shakedown into walking, this is the route to follow. Those looking for a more sporting walk, however, who don't mind steep gradients and less distinct paths, should consider tackling the variant which enjoys closer views of the sea. (A good day's outing would be to follow the variant to Hurlstone Point and return to Minehead along the official coast path.) The official way is described first.

Official Route

The South West Way starts rather inconspicuously between some historic, colour-washed cottages across the road from the sea wall just east of the harbour, about 75m past the Red Lion pub. For walkers setting out on a long-distance section (or even the entire South West Way!) this is an auspicious moment. Here is the first acorn symbol and, above the sign 'Path to North Hill', appear the details 'Porlock Weir 7½, Lynmouth 20, Combe Martin 35'.

Steps lead right, to steep zig-zags up through woods past shrubs and benches, with views through the foliage down to Minehead's harbour and, back beyond The Strand, to the sprawl of Butlin's holiday camp complex.

At the path top, turn right into a cul-de-sac lane leading through Culver Cliff Wood, mixed woodland of conifers, sycamore, sessile oak, holly and rowan. This level lane passes an Exmoor National Park sign and you bear left on a bridle path to Greenaleigh Farm and North Hill. Where the track ahead dips down, fork left (signed 'North Hill and Selworthy'), climbing gently.

Beyond rhododendrons, the steadily ascending path emerges from trees to give magnificent views across Bridgewater Bay to the South Wales coast, from Porthcawl to Penarth. 600ft. (180m) below lies a remote pebbly beach leading to Greenaleigh Point. Pass a path on the right to Burgundy Chapel (see variant) and continue climbing gradually towards the moor top. The path veers up left and reaches a junction on the summit of North Hill. (Left and sharp left both offer return loops to Minehead; straight ahead leads down Woodcombe and a slightly more circuitous return via Higher Town. In fact, hereabouts

On North Hill above Grexy Combe

are several interlinking paths, most of them made by the Luttrell family in the 19th century. They owned the whole area for hundreds of years and also stocked the woods with pheasant.)

At this path junction, the coast path turns right for Selworthy and Bossington and in 500m passes a path signed 'Rugged Cliff Top Path to Hurlstone Point' (see variant). Now on a broad moorland track, there is a marvellous sense of space and openness. Pass through a gate and along a sunken way between gorse bushes by a fence above Grexy Combe, ignoring tracks from the left. Crossing a farm road, you arrive at the access track back left (east) to the cairn and trig. point on Selworthy Beacon (1,013ft - 308m). If time and weather are favourable, this premier viewpoint over Exmoor's highest reaches and the coast is well worth the short detour. One mile (1.6km) inland stands the picturesque National Trust village of Selworthy.

The way now veers right, past a bridle path left to Lynchcombe, to meet a coast path sign at the approaches to Hurlstone Point. This was misaligned at the author's last visit. It is important not to walk on the clear path left (west) which contours round the side of Bossington Hill: the views from it are superb, but it takes you right inland to Lynch. Instead, aim down the small dry valley ahead, and at the bottom turn left onto a stony farm track which crosses a footbridge

over the wooded River Horner to the car park *(telephone)* at
BOSSINGTON. *(Bed and breakfast accommodation; snacks at The Old
Bakehouse').*

(In fact, the path down over Hurlstone Point signed 'Dangerous' is
a definitive right of way, more exhilarating, and perfectly safe with
usual care in all but the foulest weather. It zig-zags down past a
Coastguard lookout and turns left (south) to rejoin the track along to
Bossington. Unless the River Horner is in spate, it is usually possible
to avoid an inland detour altogether by walking along the beach. Look
for a twisting path down through gorse to Bossington Beach - it leaves
about 100m past the Coastguard lookout, at a stile seaward of a seat.)

Variant from Minehead

Walk to the west end of the promenade (refreshments), pass the Inshore
Rescue station and gasworks, on a path signed 'Greenaleigh Farm' which
climbs gradually in trees to the farm (Bed and Breakfast). Continuing ahead on
the level, the ruins of Burgundy Chapel on a mound are reached. Little is
known of its origins or the derivation of its name. Speculations include a votive
chapel or, more likely, a retreat for the occupants of Dunster Castle, as an
entry in the house accounts of 1405 suggests.

A very steep path climbs inland (south) towards the main coast path on
North Hill. Keep left at the first junction and straight ahead at the next, up to
the acorn signpost, turning right towards Selworthy and Bossington. In about
500m, take a yellow-waymarked path right, signed 'Rugged Cliff-Top Path to
Hurlstone Point'. A left fork is taken at the second stile, then a rough track
descends beside a marshy stream in a ravine to the bottom of the combe,
crossing it about ½ way down (not named, but map ref: 937 481). From a
point at a bend in the combe, a distinct path leads diagonally and steeply uphill
to a walled bank (National Trust boundary) which is followed seaward. Where
the wall turns left (north-west), parallel to the coast, keep by it on a plainer
path, past the site of West Myne Farm and right along to the crags of Western
Brockholes.

Here, go round the head of Henners Combe by the wall and climb over
feeder streams, keeping above scree. Once over the next valley - East Combe
-look for a path through bracken beyond a gateway; this leads towards
Hurlstone Point. Unless the weather is wild (in which case turn inland onto the
official path) go down the zig-zags past the Coastguard lookout and turn inland
onto the main route (or along the beach - see above.)

Onward Official Route

Bossington is a delightful Somerset village whose well manicured
thatched cottages have curiously tall chimneys. Walking seawards,
you pass a path left to **PORLOCK** *(shops; services; meals and refreshments; pubs; accommodation; campsite; early closing Wednesday)* and

Bossington

follow a field track round between hedges, with the imposing bulk of Bossington Hill rearing some 900ft. (274m) above, popular with hang-gliders.

The coast path turns left behind the high pebble storm beach, past limekilns and World War II pillbox ruins and along the edge of pasture over stiles and through gates, waymarked with red paint flashes. There are signs warning against bathing and using inflatables in offshore winds, and a fenced-off memorial stone to '11 Brave U.S. Airmen' who died here on October 29th 1942; otherwise, the eye is drawn inland to stretches of reedy water - a bird sanctuary frequented by many migrant species.

Past the west end of the pebble bank, the path has eroded away, committing the walker to an awkward hobble over large pebbles and boulders to reach a flight of stone steps up to the road. Turn right to arrive at the hamlet of **PORLOCK WEIR** *(Ship Inn; Anchor Hotel; cafe; car park; toilets; telephone).* Fishermen and yachtsmen use the little harbour which, up to the 1700's took in catches of herring and later saw a growing commercial trade with Wales, exporting pit-props

Porlock Weir

and produce from the Vale of Porlock. Today it's a busy place during the holiday season.

SECTION 2 - Porlock Weir to Lynmouth/Lynton;   11miles (18km)

High level, undulating woodland, subject to landslip in places but luxuriant and colourful, leads out to delightful open coast far above inaccessible, bouldery foreshore. Grassy hillside is climbed (or a more adventurous route taken past a lighthouse on rocky slopes) to hilltop Countisbury. Pleasant going parallel to the busy A39 road brings you down to Lynmouth/Lynton. Grading - moderate.

Seasonal refreshments near Culbone Church. Pub and campsite at Countisbury. Farm B&B, seasonal refreshments, toilets and Exmoor National Park Information Centre at County Gate on inland variant from Culbone.

The coast path turns up left by the Anchor Hotel (or up steps at a sign for 'Culbone' from the seafront's west end), crosses a stile and continues through fields to a muddy track and the privately owned road at Worthy. Porlock Hill is one of the steepest in England, and motorists wishing to avoid it can reach the A39 to County Gate on payment of a small toll here.

Coastal walkers pass (free!) through a white gate to the right, signed 'Culbone Church', through an arched tunnel and up steps, following waymarks up through felled woodland - a detour due to landslip. Keep right at the top junction and proceed along the broad stony tracks as it undulates beneath the oaks of Yearnor Woods. Once known at Kitnor, they have a history of sheltering outcasts, prisoners and even a leper colony in the late 16th century. Charcoal burning and oak felling flourished during the 18th and 19th centuries, leaving many signs of paths, saw and burning pits, and ruined buildings.

Suddenly, down on the right appears **CULBONE CHURCH** *(nearby refreshment hut in season; pottery).* Reputed to be the smallest intact parish church in England still holding services, it is certainly worth looking round, with informative leaflets on sale inside. Tombstones inscribed with the family name Redd may well have literary connections with the Rudds of R.D.Blackmore's *Lorna Doone.*

The official route used to climb inland up past Silcombe, Broomstreet and Yenworthy farms to the road at County Gate and thence back to the coast via Wingate Combe. In 1979, Mr. Halliday - owner of the Glenthorne Estate on whose threshold we now stand - agreed to open up a network of permissive paths as part of a land-usage deal, with the result that from 1984 the coast path has taken the line which was previously a variant. It is a superb walk through unspoilt woods, high on the wild, precipitous edge of the sea.

The old inland route is still useful if overnight accommodation is sought, since Yenworthy Farm offers bed and breakfast, and lightweight campers can ask along the way for an overnight pitch. Additionally, there is an Exmoor National Park Information Centre and exhibition at County Gate car park. *(A leaflet 'Short Walks from*

45

Culbone Church

Sessile oaks in the Glenthorne estate

County Gate - Glenthorne Estate area', with large-scale map, is available from the National Park.) The official coast path routing is described below to Wingate Combe, followed by the variant.

Official Route

At the bridge by Culbone Lodge *(pottery)* just above Culbone Church, a 3-fingered signpost (inaccurately aligned at the author's last visit) points the way towards Lynmouth. Unfortuntely, before it gets very far, a landslip has necessitated a 3½ mile (5.6km) detour inland which is, however, well waymarked red then yellow and signed 'Diverted Coastpath'. It rejoins the original path at a sign 'Yenworthy Wood', north of Sugarloaf Hill. (The South West Way Association is pressing for a reduction in the length of this detour at the time of writing.)

Landslip is a recurring problem on these steep slopes. Trees, mostly sessile oak with shallow roots, are readily dislodged by wind and heavy rain, falling across the path or starting slides of earth. Other trees and undergrowth may then take away the path in places. These wooded stretches, however, are outstandingly beautiful - quiet, verdant in spring with luxuriant ferns and grasses, streams cascading over rocky ledges and always to the north the big drop to an invisible seashore.

(A very pleasant alternative route turns off at the sign 'Pinetum',

47

and at the 2nd sign to Glenthorne Beach turns left. At the next junction go right, then left just above Glenthorne House. Now on the drive, a turreted building (once a coach house) on your left precedes an unusual lion-topped arch at a sharp bend. Go through the arch and follow the twisting, rocky path up to another path which crosses at an angle where you turn right, back onto the official routing at Handball.)

Glenthorne dates from 1820, when the Rev. Halliday from the Isle of Wight resolved to satisfy his urge to become a squire by building a mansion here with his inherited family fortune. He planted the conifers which grace the grounds today.

Various waymarks (mainly blue) and the long-distance acorn symbols lead on, with signposts to Sisters Fountain, Wingate Combe and Lynmouth. In May or June, the rhododendrons on this stage form an exotic blaze of colour. At the stream in Wingate Combe, beyond Sisters Fountain and at a sign 'Countisbury 3½', this main route and the variant meet.

Variant from Culbone

Walk through the arch of Culbone Lodge *(pottery)*, signed 'Diversion to County Gate and Silcombe', with more signposts by the stream on the left. There is now a stiff pull up through Withycombe Wood, whereafter turn left into a hedged farm road and over to Silcombe Farm in its steep combe. The sea is now temporarily out of view and earshot, but there are compensations in the form of open countryside with its animal and bird life and farming activity.

Climbing, the lane crosses Halmer and Twitchen combes before emerging at a road and Broomstreet Farm. Continue ahead downhill, through the farmyard and on along the track. Beyond a grassy section, there appear 2 signposts at a path intersection (Map ref: 811 485 - right to Sugarloaf Hill viewpoint, left a bridleway to County Gate.) Our variant keeps straight ahead, over a field, under telegraph wires and into a field track, crossing a stream and passing a barn right. Another field leads to a walled lane and Yenworthy Farm *(Bed and Breakfast)*. Turn left past the handsome farmhouse associated with Lorna Doone and walk left up the main access track.

Before the bungalows at Yenworthy Lodge ahead, turn right on a bridleway to County Gate and up onto heather moorland. (Another track to the Sugarloaf, ¾ mile - 1.2km, leaves sharp right.) In a few hundred metres, a track sharp right is part of a designated Nature Trail to Glenthorne Beach, 1¼ miles - 2km; leaflet from the information centre at County Gate. Very soon the A39 is reached at **COUNTY GATE** *(car park; summer refreshments; toilets; Exmoor National Park Information Centre open during the season, with free exhibition and shop selling maps, books and souvenirs.)* Footpaths leave here for Malmsmead (¾ mile - 1.2km) and Oare (1¾ mile - 2.8km).

The derelict wall below the car park was once the old boundary between

Exmoor from County Gate

Somerset and Devon, while to the south Badgworthy Water and Oare Water unite to form the East Lyn river against a marvellous backdrop of Exmoor, the heart of Lorna Doone country. An engraved viewing table at the far end of the car park, erected in 1985 in memory of John Peel, 'poet and essayist best known for 16 years of writing in the Daily Telegraph's 'Country Talk'', describes the evolution of the local landscape and its farming concerns.

This coast path variant leaves here, signed 'Wingate Combe 1¾ via Cosgate Hill'. Meeting the A39 again, follow it ahead, with continuing panoramas left to Exmoor's rolling moortops and combes. After walking on a wide verge, look for a turning across the road at a white gate and into a walled track. Pass through a gateway and along the edge of pasture.

At the time of writing, Two Gates signpost has an arm missing. (The path ahead is to Blackgate via Oldbarrow Hill with its 1st century Roman signal station). You turn left through a gate and into a small conifer plantation. Go over a stile and down a field edge by a wall, now heading back to the coast. Keep left down by the wall in a steep sunken groove towards the stream in Wingate Combe. Here, too, there is always the chance that the path will be blocked or diverted due to fallen trees. Accompanied by the odd yellow waymark, the path drops by the stream, crosses it and continues down over rough ground, clearly less well walked than the route thus far. At the confluence with another stream, cross over and meet a good track at a sign (left Countisbury 3½, right Sisters Fountain) now back on the official coast path, which would make a good circular route from County Gate to Culbone, and back on the variant just described.

Onward Official Route

The path now contours round from Wingate Combe through further delightful woodland, over streams and out onto open heights, with superlative coastal views in both directions which include a glimpse back to a tree-covered islet off Desolate Point known as Sir Robert's Chair and the nearing profile of Foreland Point ahead.

A cliff fall has necessitated yet another diversion, this time up an interesting crest of land between a miniature combe and the sea. In windy weather care is needed here, as the drop to the bouldery beach far below is extremely abrupt. The circular stone ruin on the way down was almost certainly once a smugglers' lookout.

The path crosses a normally dry ravine - Pudleep Gurt - and, shortly after, the tumbling stream in Swannel Combe. There is a gate at the metalled drive from Rodney in Kipscombe Combe through which we pass, walking on down the tarmac in Caddow Combe to a coast path signpost (Countisbury 1½ miles - 2.4km). The official route now climbs left round Butter Hill and on up grassy hillside towards Countisbury.

(An altogether more exciting way - unless the weather is very rough, when it is not recommended - is to walk on down the Foreland Point Lighthouse road below impressive scree slopes. Immediately before the lighthouse entrance at the road end, the path forks up left by a notice warning it is no longer maintained. As things stand at the time of writing, it is quite safe with the usual care and climbs steadily over steep, stony slopes (Lynton Shales) above a sheer drop, with increasingly fine prospects of Lynton/Lynmouth ahead. Soon after the gradient eases, the official route comes in from the left.)

Keep right up to a signpost and after more grassy ascent the path veers right, until soon Countisbury church tower is in sight. The coast path turns right here in the direction of Lynmouth, but there is the Blue Ball pub in Countisbury, next door to the National Trust's Base Camp Exmoor Centre, and walkers coming direct from Porlock Weir might well appreciate this first chance of refreshment since then. There is camping too.

Variant to Lynmouth

If time is not pressing, a more spectacular approach to Lynmouth than the normal coast path is recommended, taking in the beauty spot of Watersmeet. Go through the churchyard and from Countisbury Church turn left on the road opposite the Blue Ball pub, then right into a green lane. With a field wall on your left, you reach a grassy knoll, whereafter the path drops through woods of sessile oak down to a fishermen's path. Turn right for a short distance to emerge in front of the Lodge at **WATERSMEET** *(National Trust Information Centre; seasonal cafe)*, situated at the confluence of the East Lyn River and Farley Water.

Take the footpath up to the car park and over the road, thereafter climbing steeply to a path junction. Here keep right along high ground called Myrtleberry Cleave, followed by a drop and climb up steep zig-zags onto Lyn Cleave, thereafter contouring along above the beautiful wooded river valley. Watch carefully for a signed track right leading down steeply and twisting between houses to emerge opposite the Golden Hind restaurant in Lynmouth. An easier continuation from Watersmeet, but lacking the elevated views, lies along the riverside path. Using this high scenic variant and the official coast path to Countisbury would provide an excellent circular walk.

Official Route

The official coast path on Countisbury Common loses height before a gate (signed Watersmeet) and continues on a ledge of hillside, snaking and undulating below the busy A39 road down Countisbury Hill.

One stormy January night in 1899, Lynmouth's lifeboat - the Louisa - was unable to be launched from her home port owing to exceptionally heavy seas. She was hauled up Countisbury Hill and down Porlock Hill to Porlock Weir by a team of 18 horses to go to the aid of the 'Forrest Hall' in difficulties on Hurlstone Point. Considering the gradients involved, the weight of the vessel (3½ tons) and the foul weather, even the 10 hours taken by this desperate rescue attempt seems little short of miraculous.

A notice by the path draws attention to the earth ramparts of Countisbury Castle, an Iron Age promontory fort. Retrospective views are of impressively rugged cliffs above Sillery Sands. An inviting green path towards the beach is unusable owing to storm damage lower down, confirmed by a notice adjacent to old wartime gun positions.

It is possible to delay road walking a little by using the wall top, but for the last 180m it's a case of dodging cars and trying to avoid carbon monoxide poisoning as holiday traffic attacks the steep road hill! Well worth taking is a waymarked path off right, into woods and zig-zagging down behind the Manor House to the foreshore. Here cross the footbridge and walk into **LYNMOUTH/LYNTON** *(all shops, services and accommodation; campsite; youth hostel ½ mile (800m) inland from Lynton - see 'Useful Addresses'; Tourist Office; Exmoor Folk Museum in Lynton; Exmoor National Park Information Centre and shop on seafront; bus routes; early closing Thursday)*.

A zig-zagging pedestrian way from the pavilion links the seaside bustle of Lynmouth with its higher level and more sedate sister Lynton. Also spanning the steep slope is a fascinating water-ballasted

Sillery Sands below Countisbury Common

Lynmouth

cable railway built in 1890, which is crossed and re-crossed by the path, affording first class views of the ingenious system as well as the coast beyond.

No mention of Lynmouth can omit the tragedy which befell the village on 15th August 1952. Massive storms on Exmoor, following a protracted spell of wet weather, produced almost 10 inches (254mm) of rain in 24 hours and a huge volume of water drained into the course of the River Lyn with disasterous consequences. The raging torrent washed away entire buildings, giving occupants no chance of escape and 34 people died. The author vividly remembers being taken as a child to see the damage some days later. Boulders, tree trunks and mud choked the river bed, while those houses that remained stood ripped apart and strewn with masonry. Considerable engineering work has gone into ensuring that a similar event never happens again.

SECTION 3 - Lynmouth/Lynton to Combe Martin; 13 miles (21km)

The curious, craggy landscape in Valley of the Rocks is reached along a popular Victorian cliff walk. Woodland paths avoid road walking, whereafter the path traverses spectacular rugged cliffside before descending inland at dramatic Heddon's Mouth. The coast is regained above Sherrycombe. A sustained and steep climb ensues to the summit of the Great Hangman, highest point on the whole South West Way and a rewarding viewpoint in clear weather. The long but gentle descent on good paths finishes at Combe Martin. Grading - moderate then more difficult. Refreshments and toilets just off route at Lee Bay., Accommodation, refreshments and toilets at Hunter's Inn.

The coast path leaves Lynmouth seafront through an arch just past the National Park Information Centre and zig-zags up steeply through gardens, over the cliff railway three times, to Lynton. Turn right before the top station into North Walk, a broad and popular tarmac path established by the Victorians which, despite its tameness, nevertheless traverses fine walking terrain for ¾ mile (1.2km) 400ft (122m) above the sea. (A higher level alternative turns up right by Lynton Town Hall, climbs through the wooded grounds of Hollerday Hill, keeping ahead at a left bend and out into the open, with far-reaching views. Continue down to Valley of the Rocks and the main route).

Along above the sea on North Walk, we can reflect on the enterprise shown by individuals in the 19th century, such as Mr.Sanford who had this way cut and surfaced in 1817 - a task which even public

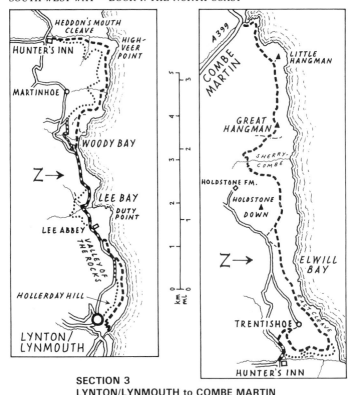

SECTION 3
LYNTON/LYNMOUTH to COMBE MARTIN

bodies in today's motorised society would baulk at. This walk was a favourite of the poet Shelley and his young bride when they stayed in Lynmouth, and before him had been visited by Coleridge and Wordsworth.

Passing the aptly named Castle Rock (or climbing up over it!), the coast path comes to grassy levels in the **VALLEY OF THE ROCKS**, surrounded by craggy outcrops. It seems likely that this curious landscape was formed during the Ice Age 10,000 years ago when the ice sheet then encasing the south-west coast forced the River Lyn to scour a drainage channel parallel to the sea instead of flowing directly into it. On a summer's weekend it is claustrophobically well visited, the human population augmented by a thriving herd of feral goats!

The official coast path routing once disappointingly took to the road for some 3 miles (4.8km) to Woody Bay. However, there are two opportunities to escape: after the small roundabout, take the second path right (the first leads to a beach), which loops round to the Lee Abbey estate fence and climbs left back to the road at the one-time toll house. (What a shame one cannot continue on the cliffs round Duty Point!)

Turn right on the road and opposite Lee Abbey itself (a church conference and holiday centre) turn left on a waymarked track signed 'Woodland Walk to Woody Bay', a longer but infinitely more pleasant alternative to the road. *(Off the road at* **LEE BAY** *below, however, are car park, toilets and tea room and the routes converge in about ½ mile (800m).*

Follow the broad woodland track, cross a stream and turn right. After a wooden footbridge, climb left immediately up steps, cross a forestry track and turn left (yellow waymark). The way now climbs and drops to regain the road which has to be walked along to the Woody Bay Hotel *(refreshments)*.

In the late 1800's considerable attempts were initiated by a Colonel Lake to develop Woody Bay as a resort. Among attractions such as a beach bathing pool, golf course and carriage drive (an alternative coast path route), was a substantial pier designed to receive paddle steamers, but within a few years it was destroyed by the sea.

From here to Hunter's Inn, the old route - though fine enough -seems unadventurous compared to the marvellous new official path closer to the sea and which is highly recommended. However, if the weather is wild, the old path is safer and is described first. (A National Trust leaflet called 'Heddon Valley and Woody Bay' gives useful information on the local path network).

Old Route

Pass the Woody Bay Hotel, go through the National Trust car park and up the often busy road to a sharp left bend. Ahead is a gate and acorned sign 'Hunter's Inn 2¼ miles' which leads you onto an old coach road through woods then out onto open cliff tops above Highveer Point, with good views all round. Turning inland above the dramatic scree-bound Heddon's Mouth Cleave, the way twists to cross Hill Brook then descends through Road Wood to the road at Hunter's Inn.

New Official Route

This high quality coastal path leaves the road just before the Woody Bay Hotel at a gate and sign right 'Public Footpath to Woody Bay

Hunter's Inn

Beach ¾ mile'. Emerging at a surfaced track by a notice 'Trees Private', turn up left, and at a sharp left bend go right, over a stile. Fork left immediately up a steep track signed to Hunter's Inn. Past gnarled trees (many of which were destroyed by a blizzard in December 1981), the good path drops gently over a stile and round past the spectacular 30ft (9m) cascade of Hollow Brook, before rising across scree and round a rocky corner in an exhilarating situation.

The path continues to climb then contour rugged heathery hillside above the sea, eventually and suddenly confronting the dramatic bastion of land at Heddon's Mouth, with its conspicuous limekiln ruin on the beach. Descending steadily, the way joins a broad path in the valley bottom turning left onto it then crossing the 2nd bridge over the Heddon's River. **HUNTER'S INN** is but a short distance to the left *(accommodation; meals; car park; cafe/gift shop; toilets; telephone).*

The hospitable and well patronized inn, with its complement of exotic peacocks, stands in a romantic setting deep in the wooded heart of Heddon's Mouth Cleave; it is the only refreshment point between Woody Bay and Combe Martin, still 8 miles of rough walking away.

Pass in front of the inn and walk along the Combe Martin road for approximately 200 yards (180m) to a gate and footpath right, signed 'Alternative path to Trentishoe Church 1½ miles - Access to Coastal Path'. This recently made and entertaining variant continues forward for some 400m into woods, then turns up left at a sign 'Trentishoe Only - Steep Path'. Unlike many ascents on the coast path, this one is well graded as it mounts almost 800ft (244m) of brackeny hillside in alpine-style zig-zags to join the current official route at the top. From just over half way up the zig-zags, a new path created by the National Trust loops seaward round Peter Rock and joins the main route on East Cleave. This is likely in the future to become the official coast path.

The present routing from Hunter's Inn continues farther along the Combe Martin road to just beyond a row of cottages, where it turns right, signed 'Trentishoe Common 2¼ miles' and 'Unfit for Motors'. A steady pull up ensues from the combe bottom until, not far short of Trentishoe church, a path leaves to the right at a National Trust Heddon Valley Estate sign - 'Combe Martin 7½ miles'. Although not strictly coastal in character, this routing does provide strong impressions of the very beautiful hinterland, with superb views back down to Hunter's Inn from the valley lip. Out of the main holiday season, the landscape imparts a distinctly Victorian flavour, as if held in suspension from the last century.

The zig-zag variant rises to join us as we continue outside an old field wall back to the coast, swinging left (south-west) on East Cleave high above the sea. Elwill Bay cliffs suffer badly from erosion and a diversion round a vanishing section of path at Bosley Gut serves as a graphic reminder of the need for vigilance in such places.

At a particularly deep and evil looking chasm, the coast path veers inland to a marker post. At a fork, keep on the upper path to the next post and follow the sign above a small combe, Neck Wood Gut, climbing gently. A broad heather ride branches off right, short-cutting the old official route which kept left here up to the Trentishoe Down road. (A little way up are possible B & B, teas and overnight camping at Holdstone Farm. To return to the coast path, take the stony track across rough moorland on Holdstone Down. In the late 1800's, a property speculator named these rough tracks 'Seaview

Road' and 'Beach Road' in an abortive attempt to develop the land.)

Farther along the track at a white acorn symbol on a rock, the coast path veers left into the substantial valley of Sherrycombe. Passing through a wall gap on the right you follow signs along the edge of the combe inland, with the massive bulk of the Great Hangman - already seen from afar and anticipated as an obstacle to be reckoned with -now looming ahead.

The path drops steeply into Sherrycombe and is very boggy in places. Once over the stream footbridge, mind and body must be steeled against the climb ahead, for the summit of the **GREAT HANGMAN,** at 1043ft (318m), is the highest point on the entire South West Way, and you start not far above sea level. The climb may be a stiff one, but is a 'once for all' effort, unlike far more strenuous stretches further south where big climbs and drops follow in quick succession.

Steep zig-zags (starting inland) assail the rugged slopes of Girt Down as height is gained. Bear left at a bench up by a wall and at its top corner continue ahead. (Walkers with time to spare can detour right to the Blackstone viewpoint for an exciting coastal panorama.) The author has never had the good fortune to arrive on the Great Hangman in clear visibility - on most occasions quite the contrary! Prospects from the great sprawling cairn are said to be far-reaching, from south and east Exmoor, the nearer coast and Holdstone Down to distant Dartmoor and, in the west, Lundy Island.

Leaving ½-left and over a stile, the coast path goes gently downhill through gorse, veering right to stay outside a field fence. The Little Hangman grows increasingly conspicuous as a pointed eminence ahead as height is lost, and at a stile can be reached by walking right. Over grass (on either of two paths), the way reaches a bench, whereafter the mile-long straggle of Combe Martin is in sight below. At at signpost, veer up left (straight on is to Wild Pear Beach) and pass a refreshment hut on the left. As if signifying the approach of civilisation after a long section of gloriously unfettered walking, the undulating path is now held tightly between field fence and clifftop hedgerow. From a shelter, the right (unmarked) path is visually more rewarding, though the official route swings left through a gate and down steps to the car park at **COMBE MARTIN** (*all shops, services and accommodation; campsites 1 mile ahead on path; Exmoor National Park Information Centre with accommodation list; car park; toilets; telephone; bus route; early closing Wed.*)

Exmoor National Park and the National Trust produce leaflets on suggested walks, giving information about the area which, to the east, is good day-walking country. This is the western perimeter of the National Park and the end of 36 miles (58km) of conscientious waymarking under its auspices.

Silver and lead mining brought some prosperity to Combe Martin from the 14th to the 19th century; also, several ambitious schemes to enclose the harbour and bring in the railway were mooted but never materialised. The village is often a welcome stopover for the coastal walker but, its surprising length apart, is largely without distinction.

SECTION 4 - Combe Martin to Woolacombe; 12 miles (19km)

A combination of road and tracks is followed by a recently opened headland path of good quality. Verges and pavement lead down to the outskirts of Ilfracombe, but the path climbs over a 450ft (136m) hilltop with marvellous views before descending direct to Ilfracombe harbour. The town is the largest since Minehead and possesses many interesting features. At first on rocky cliffs, the route takes to the old unmade coast road dropping gently to Lee village. A switchback of grassy ups and downs, many equipped with steps, brings you past Bull Point lighthouse, but the going levels off round Morte Point. Grassy slopes lead easily round to Woolacombe. Grading – moderate but more difficult in places. Campsites near Combe Martin. Meals, refreshments, accommodation, shop, toilets and buses at Hele Bay. All shops, services and accommodation at Ilfracombe. Campsite, pub, shop at Morthoe.

Leaving Combe Martin, the way turns right down Newberry Road, across from a remarkably fine old fisherman's cottage above the beach cafe ahead. Walk along below a terrace of balconied Victorian houses, following the lane (actually the coast road until 1919 when a landslip necessitated building the present highway) as it bends right uphill and rejoins the busy A399 near Sandway Caravan and Camping Park.

The next ½ mile (800m) is as unpleasant and dangerous a stretch of road walking as you will find anywhere on Britain's long-distance paths; although moves are afoot to alleviate the situation, at the time of writing they are not imminent. The road twists uphill with no pavement to Sandy Cove Hotel where, with some relief, the walker can turn off right on the erstwhile coast road, now an unmade track along above Golden Cove (access path closed in 1980 due to serious erosion) and through the edge of Bamants Wood round Napps Hill.

Just before reaching a tarred lane *(campsite reception/shop up left)*, go right over a stile and down across a field to Napps campsite, skirting

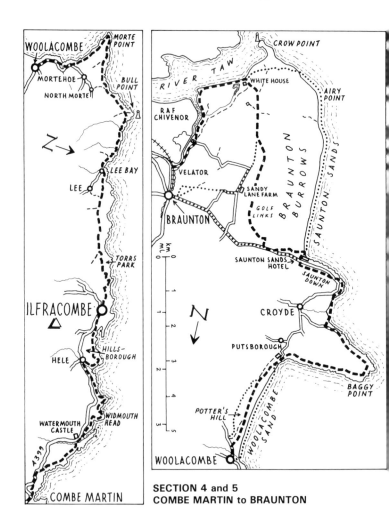

**SECTION 4 and 5
COMBE MARTIN to BRAUNTON**

its edge to meet the road near Watermouth Castle. This ramparted edifice dates from 1825 and seems unashamedly dedicated to providing fun for all the family, in one form or another!

Passing a caravan site, you are temporarily hemmed in by fences alongside the road, but after 30m escape is at hand - if the tide is out! It is then possible to turn right down the slipway onto Watermouth Bay beach, a fine natural inlet for the pleasure craft which throng it in summer. Walk out along the foreshore and look for a flight of steps left, leading up to a roadside path through woods. (If the tide is high, stay on the road for a further 25m and cross a stile to join this same path.) Eastbound walkers look at the state of tide before deciding.

Threading through plane trees just below the main road, the coast path turns down right, crosses a stream, then encircles Widmouth Head on a recently opened section of excellent quality, fully justifying the fight to obtain access. Although there are some sharp undulations and flights of steps which demand concentration, views are worth pausing for, since they form the last retrospective glimpses of the Great Hangman and Watermouth Bay.

Here there is a growing sense of intimacy with the sea itself, encountered at close quarters, which makes one aware of how remote above the water's edge has been the walking on much of the route so far.

Beyond Samson's Bay, the path turns right over a stile and along by a wall seaward of the road. Descending gently through bracken, it then climbs to a row of coastguard cottages at the road, separated from it at first by a wall, then surrendering to the grass verge and ultimately onto pavement down to the outskirts of Ilfracombe at **HELE BAY** *(cafe; restaurant; pub; shop; toilets; buses.)*

At the Hele Bay pub, turn right down Beach Road to the seafront, past the public toilets and up steps. Ilfracombe lies the other side of the prominence called Hillsborough and the path now climbs determinedly (ignore a left turn signed Ilfracombe). After the first bend, cross a path and mount steps opposite to detour a landslip, continuing on up to a viewpoint and iron railing. Still climbing, the route reaches Hillsborough's summit at 447ft (136m) and starts descending - well walked and with continuing marvellous views of Ilfracombe's harbour.

Turn right just before the public park, then left down the side of a Pitch and Putt course. Pass the public toilets and turn right along to **ILFRACOMBE** *(all shops, services and accommodation; youth hostel; Tourist Office; museum; boat trips; bus routes etc; early closing Thurs.).*

Ilfracombe is the largest town encountered since Minehead and

Ilfracombe Harbour

some walkers will doubtless wish to spend time here exploring and enjoying its ameneties. A fishing port since medieval times, with a splendid natural harbour, Ilfracombe became established as an exclusive resort during the mid 1800's. Later, increasing public transport - especially the railway and channel steamers - encouraged visitors of all social classes and boarding houses proliferated, becoming as much a part of the town's character as the grand hotels. In common with many British resorts, Ilfracombe's fortunes have changed, precipitated perhaps by the closure of both its railway and steamer services over the past decade and a half (although the latter still operate at times during the summer season).

Nevertheless, the town is certainly not without charm. Among sights of interest are Lantern Hill above the harbour, with its restored 14th century St.Nicholas Chapel; the George and Dragon pub dating from 1360; an excellent museum; Capstone Parade leading to the Victoria Pavilion and Gardens; and the famous Tor's Walk which the coast path route utilises as it takes its leave of the town.

In fact, finding the way out of Ilfracombe is not straightforward, the correct route depending, as the joke goes, upon where you start from! Aim north-west towards the sea from the town centre, and from Granville Road walk up Tors Walk Avenue, turning right at a waymarked telegraph pole. Beyond the buildings, turn left onto the coastal path then right, down to a delightful level path along the cliffside.

Zig-zags lead up to the cliff top where you keep left before swinging round right and dropping along a field bottom, over a stile and on between rocky outcrops. Soon the way descends into a shallow valley and rises to meet the old unmade coast road emerging from Langleigh Lane.

Climbing gently and levelling off over sheep pasture above Flat and Shag Points, the track becomes a tarred lane at a gate and bungalow *(free-range eggs and camping at North Warcombe Farm to the left, also the footpath to Lee village)*. Keep ahead at a left bend, towards distant Bull Point, and at the steep lane bottom turn right to **LEE** *(Smugglers Bar and Bistro open all day for coffees, teas, bar food; hotel and licensed restaurant; car park; toilets; early closing Sat.)*.

Walk up the steep lane out of Lee and turn right through a gate at a National Trust sign for Damage Cliff, following a fence round the cliff edge. After crossing the stream at Hilly Mouth, there is a stiff pull up a stepped slope onto Damaghue Cliff, followed by another down and up over Bennett's Mouth. Grassy clifftops bring you abruptly above and unexpectedly close to Bull Point lighthouse (afternoon visits), rebuilt inland after a major cliff fall in September 1972 threatened the land beneath it. In dubious visibility (not necessarily dense fog!) the foghorn is liable to sound, and the author can guarantee that warning

Lee Bay

notices to this effect are not superfluous.

Go down left of the boundary wall, cross the lighthouse access road and keep forward along above the shoreline. More steep steps lead downhill, whereafter keep right by gorse to a waymark post. Cross the stream at the back of Rockham Beach and pass a gate left leading to North Morte Farm Caravan and Camping Site. Cross the stile at a National Trust sign and turn left uphill, then down into the next combe (if in doubt hereabouts, just stay along the cliff edge.) Before the stream, a path left contours along to **MORTEHOE** village *(pub, shop; Post Office; telephone.)* After the stream there is yet another stepped zig-zag ascent, with views back across remarkable rock reefs stacked like silver wafers, especially impressive at low tide.

Walking out now towards Morte Point, take a right fork to stay by the cliff edge and pass a bench and path off left. The way now levels off at no great height above the waves and suddenly you come round the tip of the rocky promontory itself, with the great sweep of Woolacombe Bay and Baggy Point ahead.

Offshore rocks and currents not only look menacing, but the Morte Stone - Rock of Death - has taken its toll of sail-driven shipping in previous centuries. Indeed, so inhospitable is its coast that wrecking - the luring of vessels onto rocks by showing misleading lights and other strategies - reputedly proved more profitable, if more lethal, than smuggling.

Barricane Beach, Woolacombe

The coast path grows grassier as it heads south-east, keeping right below buildings and the road, then meeting the latter, short-cutting a bend and finally entering by its grass-flanked seafront the holiday town of **WOOLACOMBE** *(all shops, services and accommodation; bus route; early closing Wed./Sat.).*

After so many miles spent walking on clifftops, it is exhilarating to encounter a real beach - 2 miles of golden sands fringed with Atlantic breakers. A hundred years ago, Woolacombe was just a farmstead and a few workers' cottages but by the early 1900's had already developed into a popular resort. Too exposed for fishing, smuggling or even an effective lifeboat, Woolacombe's great attraction for holidaymakers has been its magnificent foreshore.

SECTION 5 - Woolacombe to Braunton (via Crow Point); 14 miles (23km)

Long sands and a field-edge circuit of Baggy Point headland takes you to Croyde beach and level walking above the road to Saunton Sands. Short cut variants to Braunton will reduce mileage if necessary, but the official path, though poorly defined, skirts the vast dune system of Braunton Burrows to reach the River Taw's estuary banks which are followed in to Braunton. Alternative beach walk along Saunton Sands. Few gradients throughout this section.   Grading - moderate to easy.

Seasonal refreshments and a hotel at Putsborough. Shops, accommodation, pub, campsite and buses at Croyde, just off route. Hotel and seasonal refreshments at Saunton Sands.

Provided the tide is not right up and that weather conditions are reasonable, walking the length of Woolacombe Sands is easy on both feet and eyes; the surface is firm and there is a vivid sense of being suspended between ocean and dry land in a world full of light and distance. At the far end after passing a conspicuous house ('Vention') at the start of Putsborough Sand (popular with surfers), make for the beach cafe half way up the rocks. Stone steps lead up to a car park, where turn right, passing some public conveniences and climbing the bank ahead to cross a stile.

(There are two other ways to reach Putsborough from Woolacombe: an unofficial, more elevated romp over Potters Hill (National Trust) and Woolacombe Down, or the normal high tide route. This latter starts on the road south from Woolacombe Warren. It is signposted and meets Marine Drive after some 800m (although it is possible to continue ahead before having

The walk along Woolacombe Sands

to descend to beach level at Black Rock). Marine Drive becomes a track leading out near the Putsborough Sands Hotel (open to non-residents), 200m beyond which is a stile on the right. Walk through here to join the beach alternative.)

Angling uphill on cattle pasture, there are increasingly fine views over the graceful crescent of Woolacombe Bay right back to Morte Point. At first outside the clifftop field wall, the coast path enters National Trust property and proceeds along the edges of fields. It is pleasant walking and soon **BAGGY POINT** is rounded. Passing through a gate a stony farm track is reached, but at the Point itself, although the marvellous prospect ahead across Bideford Bay can be distracting, look to the right for the lower path which offers much better sea views and is no longer in distance. Baggy Point is a prime site for birdwatching, especially during the nesting and migrating seasons.

Shortly beyond a collection of bones from a whale washed ashore in 1915 and installed for posterity by the National Trust on a grassy bank, you meet a tarred lane. This leads down past cream tea signs, round by a slipway and inland a little past Ruda Park camping and caravanning site. Turn right down past a beach shop to the sands *(toilets)*, but if the tide is high it may be necessary to divert half a mile inland to **CROYDE** *(some shops; pub; accommodation; campsite; buses for Barnstaple; early closing Wednesday.)*

On the normal beach route - incidentally a very popular venue for

Whalebones near Croyde

surfing - cross the stream mouth and climb from the south end of the sands onto low cliffs outside cultivated fields. The path soon veers left up past a hotel and other buildings, crosses the Croyde to Saunton road (B3231) and continues along above it with magnificent views ahead stretching to Hartland Point.

After almost a mile of level walking on the flanks of Saunton Down, Saunton Sands Hotel is approached, a vast white building visible retrospectively for many a mile ahead. Dropping to the road and crossing it, the coast path is reluctantly hemmed in between tennis courts, putting green and the cliff edge. Steps lead down to the beach where decisions must be taken regarding the next leg of the route.

In order to reach Appledore and Westward Ho! the other side of the Taw and Torridge rivers, it is necessary to walk inland via Barnstaple, a total distance of 27 miles (43km) along the estuary shore. On 2nd April 1987, the Environment Minister William Waldegrave officially opened a new stretch of footpath/cycleway between Barnstaple and Bideford, based on the disused railway line which Devon County Council purchased from British Rail in 1985. Before that date, walkers

Braunton Burrows from Saunton Down

faced a monotonous tramp, much of it on roads. Even today, the combination of railway trackbed walking, first from Braunton to Barnstaple (previously a gap in the path) then from Barnstaple to Bideford, will not be to everyone's liking despite its being quiet and through pleasant surroundings. For those desiring rapid progress here, frequent buses run along to Barnstaple and out to Westward Ho! where the path is truly coastal again.

From Saunton Sands, our first objective is Braunton village, which can be reached in three ways:-

1) Walking direct along the road is feasible in pressing circumstances, but is not recommended owing to heavy, fast traffic.

2) The true (though unofficial) coastal route: except at high tide, it is possible to walk the length of Saunton Sands (4 miles - 6.5km). To landward is **BRAUNTON BURROWS,** an extensive area of sand dunes rising to 100ft. (30m) and of great interest to botanists and ornithologists. The dunes habitat is, of course, vulnerable to wind damage so wooden palings have been installed to trap blowing sands. Large sections of the Burrows have been planted with marram grass whose roots bind together and stabilise the topography, while in places paths are reinforced with old railway sleepers.

Inland, hollows filled with fresh water and known as 'slacks' or 'pans' are home for many rare plant species and numerous insects. Small mammal inhabitants include foxes and rabbits (once bred commercially here) and the sandy soil also attracts lizards and snails. The Burrows is a favoured resting ground for migrant birds, especially during the autumn.

When looking for a way off the beach near its southern end, don't be tempted by a track heading towards South Burrow Cottage. Instead, continue round Airy Point where a change of direction reveals Appledore across the estuary. Avoid going too far to Crow Point itself but take a timber-slatted bridlepath north of east. Old lighthouses near the path have long since disappeared, replaced by a new structure on Crow Point. A rough road leads on to White House, once associated with an Appledore ferry which, if still in service, would save the coastal walker considerable footwork!

A good embankment path is now followed round the south and east of Horsey Island whose peace is periodically shattered by jets taking off and landing at RAF Chivenor; if you don't mind the noise, it is quite exciting standing so close beneath their flight paths. Beyond the Toll House (for driving out to White House), a man-made channel bypasses the twisting Caen River and allows ships access to Velator, Braunton's little port. Once across Velator Bridge, you reach the disused railway line at a level crossing, turning right along the trackbed.

3) Now for the 'official' routing from Saunton Sands which, it has to be said, is less than satisfactory at the time of writing. It is, however, the best option if the tide is high:

From the beach below Saunton Sands Hotel, turn left up past the Surf Life Saving Club to a public car park *(shop)*. Walk up the access road and turn off right, opposite some garages. The path passes ancient holiday chalets, proceeds along outside gardens then meets the road. Turn right on it for some 500m, noting tiny St. Anne's chapel, and just beyond Saunton Golf Club turn right down a lane at a waymarked telegraph pole. Where the lane bends left, keep ahead through a gate and aim ½-left for a groove between two hillocks which leads to a gate. Turn left here on a sandy track and be prepared for some navigational difficulties ahead!

The official path - marked on most guides - takes a very poor line and is completely non-existent on the ground in places. The short cut east to Sandy Lane Farm, for example, lies through impenetrable thickets with no stiles in evidence at the farm end. Caught between Golf Club interests and governmental apathy, the routing is obscure and badly needs clarification and waymarking. The author's advice, and that of the South West Way Association, is to keep to the eastern edge of the golf links, following what waymarks there are. This is not as simple as it sounds but with luck you will pick up a broad, rutted road leading south (the so-called American Road). In a mile or so, fork left to arrive at White House and the beach route which you follow into Braunton.

A short cut to Braunton is possible by turning left (north) on the American Road at map ref: 464 346. Turn right by a gas bottling plant (the erstwhile Sandy Lane Farm), then shortly after an acute left bend go right over a stile and along a field edge. Half-way along, cross a stile into the adjacent field and at the end turn left to the corner and right between fields, now heading for Marwood's conspicuous church on its distant hill.

Great Field, as this area is known, was once a fine surviving example of medieval strip cultivation but is rapidly succumbing to modern farming techniques. Turn right, then left onto a firm track and into '2nd Field Lane' bungalow estate. (Contrary to County Council waymarking, the official line crosses a stile by a brick pillar box, skirts the cricket pitch, crosses the road, follows Mile Stile to the river bridge, turns right and reaches the railway trackbed, thus bypassing Braunton village.) From the bungalows however, turn right on the main road and enter **BRAUNTON** *(all shops, services and accommodation; buses to Barnstaple; early closing Wednesday.)*

SECTION 6 - Braunton to Westward Ho! via Barnstaple, Instow and Appledore;   17 miles (27km)

A long, flat walk mostly on dismantled railway track to get round the Taw estuary. First 6 miles (9.5km) past RAF Chivenor to Barnstaple, then a further 7 miles (11km) to Instow. A seasonal ferry to Appledore (or a walk via Bideford) leads on to Northam Burrows Countryside Park and a 2 mile (3.2km) trudge along a pebble ridge to Westward Ho! Walkers wishing to reduce some (or all) of this uninspiring stage can use the frequent bus service between Braunton, Barnstaple and Westward Ho!   Grading - easy.
All shops, services and accommodation at Barnstaple. Ditto at Instow (youth hostel), Bideford, Appledore and Westward Ho! (campsite).

To reach the disused railway track in Braunton, turn right towards Velator, first left then right on Station Road to a stile and the coast path routing ahead.

Available for use by walkers but not yet officially designated, the trackbed of the old Barnstaple to Ilfracombe railway (closed 1970) takes you straightforwardly if undramatically the 6 or so miles (9.5km)

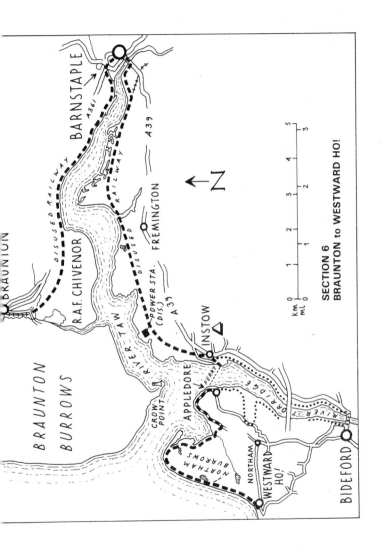

SECTION 6
BRAUNTON to WESTWARD HO!

to Barnstaple. RAF Chivenor's bustle gives way to more genuinely estuarine scenery from Heanton Court onwards, but there is an inauspicious ending opposite Barnstaple Rugy Football Club's grandstand. A white gate leads into a narrow lane past a works on the right, whereafter fork right into Mill Lane. Go next right, then left when you emerge onto Rolle Quay by its inn. Once on the main road, walk past the bus station, turn right over the bridge and enter the centre of **BARNSTAPLE** (all shops, services and accommodation; St. Anne's Chapel and North Devon Athenaeum museums; Castle Mound opposite the Civic Centre; Pannier Market on Tuesdays and Fridays; BR station for main line connections at Exeter; buses ahead to Instow, Appledore and Westward Ho! early closing Wednesday.)

More disused railway lies ahead - 7 miles (11.25km) to Instow - and once again an option to take the bus can be exercised, either to Instow or as far as Westward Ho! itself, back on the coast proper.

To leave Barnstaple, cross the River Taw on Long Bridge (A39 for Bideford) and turn right through a furniture factory premises. Pass various piles of gravel and timber and a car park and walk out above the river saltings. In a further 500m, the railway trackbed is joined at a coast path sign; it closed as recently as 1982, hence its depiction on many maps as still operational or not yet dismantled.

Perhaps because you are heading seaward again, this stretch of trackbed tramping seems to hold the key to better country ahead. After the crossing of Fremington Pill, once a busy quay, fields to the right are replaced by saltwater marsh as you approach disused Welland Power Station. A long curve south brings you round past Instow Sands into the mouth of the Torridge and **INSTOW** (shops and services; pubs; cafes; youth hostel; buses for Barnstaple and Appledore/Westward Ho! early closing Wednesday).

From Spring Bank Holiday to mid-September, a ferry plies between Instow and Appledore every 20 mins. - 3 hours either side of high water. However, more good railway path continues from Instow's old signal box and level crossing to Bideford, passing beneath the new and controversial road bridge (no footway). Outside ferry operating times, an onward walking route is thus available, though it is not otherwise recommended.

At the southern end of the railway path (about 3 miles - 4.8km), proceed along the main road for 150m to the river bridge in **BIDEFORD** (all shops, services and accommodation; buses for Appledore and Westward Ho! early closing Wednesday). The town's shady quay-sides are quiet today but were once some of England's busiest. There is a statue of Charles Kingsley, perhaps best remembered for his book

Westward Ho!

The next 2½ miles (4km) to Appledore is followed by 4½ miles (7.2km) round Northam Burrows to Westward Ho! Whilst purists may scorn any hint of evasion, some walkers will by now be chafing at the bit for some 'real' coast! If you belong to the latter category, a bus to Westward Ho! is the quickest; by foot on B roads via Silford is most direct (about 2½ miles - 4km).

The full forward route uses existing definitive rights of way and leaves Bideford north along the quay, going inland behind the West of England Building Society, a bus depot and a now defunct boatyard. Walk beneath the new road bridge inland of Chircombe House and turn right down a narrow lane back to the river bank. Footpath signs lead on along Lower Cleave, then you fork right and right again to the National Trust sign 'Burrough Farm'. Another right turn over stepping stones brings you to an inland diversion (signed Northam ¾) to the road, regaining the riverside path at Appledore Shipyard via Bloody Corner and Wooda. This diversion is due to sea wall damage and may be modified following a public enquiry. Now continue past Dockside, the Bell Inn and a glove factory, turning right into Myrtle Street and left onto the Quay (where the Instow ferry would land you) at **APPLEDORE** *(some shops and services; cafes; pubs; accommodation; Maritime Museum, early closing Wednesday).* It is a delightful place in which to linger, long associated with shipbuilding which still to this day employs many hundred people and currently specialises in dredgers. During the Elizabethan era, Appledore grew in importance and was heavily involved in the herring fishing industry for many years. The port was well known for its fine schooners so it is appropriate that such replicas as the 'Golden Hind' and the 'Nonsuch' were built here for filming and television work.

Keep right of the Lifeboat House (inshore rescue boat - the main craft is moored in the estuary) and into a path ending at Hinks Boatyard. Turn first right up the road and either stay on it to Westward Ho! or walk round Northam Burrows. At the time of writing, this 'Countryside Park' is blighted by rubbish tip land reclamation, so check the wind direction before choosing your way!

Farther on you are at the northern end of a 2 mile (3.2km) pebble ridge outside the Royal North Devon golf links. Walking is easiest on the beach itself, but at high tide the best must be made of a bad job! Not only is this 20ft. (6m) high ridge troublesome to walkers, it is vulnerable to westerly gales and thus a constant worry to the local council whose responsibility it is to stabilise the shifting pebbles.

After a long and somewhat uninspiring section round the estuaries,

The Pebble Ridge, Westward Ho!

coastal walking of the highest quality now lies ahead....but first, **WESTWARD HO!** *(all shops, services and accommodation; campsite; buses; early closing Wednesday).*

Uniquely named after Charles Kingsley's novel, Westward Ho! was developed in the 1860's, though less successfully than had been hoped: Charles Kingsley himself was unenthusiastic! In 1874 the United Services College was established, an alternative to traditional public school for young aspiring officers, including Rudyard Kipling. (It moved nearer London 30 years later and the building is now a terrace of flats.) In the 1870's there was a 500ft-long pier, but the seas on this exposed coast made short work of destroying it. Today Westward Ho! seems dedicated to fast food and entertainment, a brash, slightly tawdry resort which most coastal walkers will welcome only for its chance of refreshment. Indeed, supplies and arrangements for accommodation ahead should be carefully looked at as the next stages of the walk are less well provided with amenities.

A seawater swimming pool and impressive rock reefs attract attention, but the real offshore interest lies in Middle Stone Age relics found here under a layer of peat. Amongst them were flint tools, shells, animal bones and deer antlers, all well preserved.

CHAPTER 2
Westward Ho! to Newquay
(98 miles - 158km)

More strenuous walking on rougher paths leads to beautiful clifftop woods past Buck's Mills hamlet and along the Hobby Drive to the fishing village of Clovelly - a much visited Devon showpiece. Supplies and refreshments become progressively harder to obtain as the coast path rounds Hartland Point and embarks on one of the South West Way's wildest and toughest sections. Superb cliff scenery accompanies you the whole way to Bude, with only Hartland Quay and off-route Morwenstow offering any respite from the elements and a long series of big combes which are crossed on fierce gradients.

Bude faces Atlantic rollers and is famous for surfing. More wave-ravaged coast leads on, with further considerable climbs and drops in store for the walker. Topping the Dizzard and High Cliff, you pass Pentargon waterfall and arrive at Boscastle. Varied and scenic clifftop walking of high quality takes you to Tintagel with its island castle and King Arthur associations. Summer crowds, however, are soon left behind for wonderful and remote coast, first above old slate quarries, then along another switchback of steep-sided valleys to Port Isaac.

Fine walking past coves and headlands brings you out to Pentire Point above the Camel estuary, providing exhilarating views in all directions. Easier going now follows through the family resort of Polzeath and along the Camel's sandy shores to the Padstow ferry.

Rounding Stepper Point, opposite Pentire Point at the River Camel's mouth, you take in a succession of popular little sandy bays between low, rocky promontories. Passing Bedruthan Steps is a highlight of this section before the long sweep of Watergate Bay announces the transition from unspoiled and largely uninhabited coastline to the urban holiday centre of Newquay.

SECTION 7 - Westward Ho! to Clovelly;   12 miles (19km)

Tougher gradients and terrain than encountered thus far start soon after leaving Westward Ho! as the path drops and climbs, first along open coast then through beautiful clifftop woodland. Buck's Mills hamlet punctuates this wild section, followed by undulating fields and a long walk on the unique Hobby Drive, a stony carriageway winding through magnificent

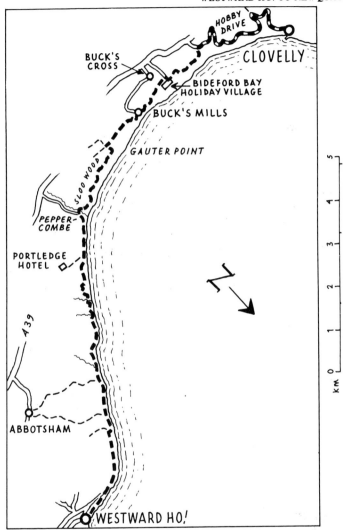

SECTION 7
WESTWARD HO! to CLOVELLY

woods to emerge at the top end of Clovelly.   Grading - more difficult.
Seasonal refreshments, B&B at Buck's Mills, also telephone.

Customised chalets line the exit from Westward Ho!. beyond which
the path keeps ahead (right) and soon joins the trackbed of yet another
railway, though not for long! Opened in 1901 and never connected to
the main rail network, the Bideford to Appledore line closed just 16
years later, when its rolling stock was shipped to France for war
service.

Where the railway embankment veers inland at a fence, the coast
path undulates along low sandstone and shale cliffs above spectacular
rock platforms. Buck's Mills and Clovelly are visible as pale specks on
the wooded sweep of Bideford Bay. Near the second of two well used
footpaths inland to Abbotsham is the remains of Greencliff lime-kiln,
after which you climb Cockington Cliff and drop to cross a stream
right at beach level. For long-distance walkers who started at
Minehead, this is some of the toughest terrain encountered so far. The
bouldery beach is strewn with driftwood and jetsam, but what was
once a steep scramble up the other side has been mercifully provided
with steps and a handrail. Proposals for a wooden viaduct here were
dropped for economy reasons.

More leg work on considerable gradients brings you out to open cliff
at Higher Rowden and a descent to Portledge Mouth, a secluded
beach. A track leads up to the Portledge Hotel but the mansion itself,
home of the Coffin family for 800 years, is hidden in its lovely wooded
valley.

At last the more wooded section of coast is approached below
Peppercombe. Beyond a stile there stands an impressive ruin by a
large beech tree and a lane leading to Peppercombe Farm. Immediately opposite the entrance to Castle Bungalow, turn sharp left and
climb into woodland, passing momentarily through a field containing
traces of Peppercombe Castle, an Iron Age hill fort. The subsequent
walk through Sloo Wood is sheer delight as the path undulates
through sessile oak and birch, bluebells carpeting the ground in May.
Other wildflowers in evidence include foxgloves, primroses, campions
and numerous ferns.

At Gauter Pool there is a sharp left turn inland over double stiles,
followed by a green track and two more stiles to Worthygate, whereafter you are in a hedged farm track to the right along the ridge. It
narrows to a path winding down past a Coastguard lookout to emerge
at the hamlet of **BUCK'S MILLS** *(General Store/cafe - May to September; telephone; limited B&B accommodation; campsite a mile inland.)*

Clovelly from the Hobby Drive

The hamlet itself was once the exclusive domain of the Braund family, dark, swarthy people quite unlike other Devonians and thought to have descended from survivors of a Spanish Armada galleon. It is worth walking down to the beach to see the lime-kilns in which Pembrokeshire limestone was burned to sweeten local fields. One of the kilns resembles a ruined castle, with buttresses and a circular 'keep'. Devoid of car parking space and thus quite unspoiled, the settlement is tastefully picturesque but supports few permanent inhabitants; its tiny population is swelled by second-home owners and holidaymakers during the summer season.

The coast path leaves Buck's Mills seaward of the store and climbs steeply in woods, then along field edges to the Bideford Bay Holiday Village access road. Turn sharp right at a warmarked telegraph pole and left in front of the Bay View Stores/Off Licence. Rounding a field edge, you will pass a noxious rubbish dump, memory of which is quickly erased by walking round its back, down steeply and on along in very pleasant surroundings.

A stile is crossed and at the field top ahead, turn left to a gateway and stile. There are dramatic views right, towards the coastal headlands beyond Clovelly. Having crossed the stile, angle down left by a fence (not ahead through a gap in a bank), go right over the little stream bridge, climb steps and turn right onto the Hobby Drive.

Whether it was actually built by Napoleonic prisoners of war or by Clovelly fishermen during hard times, its construction was the 'hobby' of Sir James Hamlyn-Williams who owned the Clovelly Estate in the early 1800's. A newer section made to bypass landslips is marked by a stone bench inscribed: 'The new portion of road measuring 833 yards was added to the Hobby by Frederick and Christine Hamlyn in the year of our Lord God 1901'.

This stretch of the walk, on a good stony surface and through majestic woods, has its drawbacks. Even if you are spared the passage of motor vehicles (from a toll house on the A39), the way to Clovelly -tantalisingly glimpsed now and again - can seem endless as the Hobby loops in huge hidden dog-legs round a series of combes. Eventually however, you reach the top of a path leading down to **CLOVELLY** *(General Store/Post Office; cafe; 2 pubs (food) - the New Inn on the main street and the Red Lion by the jetty; accommodation; Visitor Centre and car park; early closing Saturday).*

The coast path continues ahead, but most walkers will wish to visit this showpiece Devon village. It will entail a sharp descent and subsequent climb back up the cobbled street amongst thronging sightseers - a disincentive for those carrying heavy rucksacks, although the opportunity to obtain supplies and refreshments on this increasingly

Clovelly Harbour

wild coast will be hard to resist. Actually, Clovelly is best before 10.00am. when the coach parties and day-trippers begin to flood in, or after 5.00pm. when they are leaving.

The original jetty forming Quay Pool was built around 1600 by the Carys of Clovelly Court, Lords of the Manor for 400 years. By 1800, Clovelly's importance as a herring fishing port was already giving way to tourism, fuelled by the writings of Charles Dickens and Charles Kingsley. The Hamlyns, a London banking family who acquired the estate in 1730, retain control to this day and it may be due to their stewardship that the village has not succumbed to commercial exploitation on any significant scale.

The inhabitants of Clovelly live a rather public life, open to the scrutiny of thousands of visitors who risk twisted ankles and broken heels on the stepped and cobbled High Street. Wheeled transport has never penetrated here, all goods being transported by sledge and donkey, with the exception of the quayside area near the motorable back road.

The powerful lifeboat is moored conspicuously offshore, witness to ferocious weather which can threaten shipping on this treacherous coast. In 1821, 24 local boats sank in a gale and 31 lives were lost. 17 years later another 21 drowned in a similar disaster.

SECTION 8 - Clovelly to Hartland Quay (or Hartland); 11 miles (18km)

The beginning of an increasingly remote and strenuous section of coastal walking, though nothing too serious before Hartland Quay. Pleasant woodland paths from Clovelly offer various alternatives before ups and downs over attractive stream valleys give way to level walking along field edges, mostly through National Trust land. Skirting an M.O.D. Radar Station, you reach the lighthouse and clifftop at Hartland Point - one of the South West Way's major headlands. Passing dramatic rock folding, the path threads its way above rugged, wave-lashed cliffs, down and up through combes, finally reaching the lane to Hartland (inland) or down to Hartland Quay. Grading - more difficult.
Seasonal refreshments at Hartland Point car park.

NOTE: For walkers on the coast path, Clovelly signifies the start of a 24 mile (39km) stretch of magnificently rugged and remote coast running down to Bude. The next supply point is Bude itself, though seasonal refreshments are available at Hartland Quay and Morwenstow. Although it begins easily enough, the walking grows ever more strenuous and from Hartland Quay onwards will tax even the fittest at

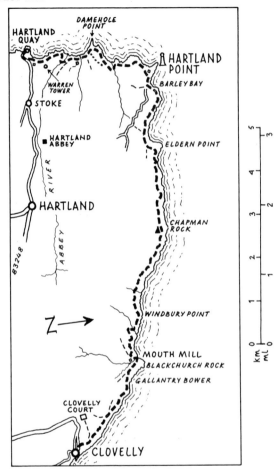

SECTION 8
CLOVELLY to HARTLAND QUAY

The 'Angel Wings' shelter

times. It is wise therefore to allow plenty of time and to carry adequate energy rations. In rough weather, Hartland Quay to Bude can turn into a formidable endurance test, though *in extremis* you can escape inland at one or two points.

From the top of Clovelly where the coast path emerges from the Hobby Drive keep ahead right, slightly downhill on the road and turn right at a bend by a large tree. Cross another road (Clovelly's back road), go through a gate and into the grounds of Clovelly Court. (Alternatively, from the village turn right just above the Doctor's surgery, go up North Hill and Backstairs. Steps lead to Mount Pleasant and the road near the Clovelly Court gates.)

After 200m on the broad track, take a right fork (concessionary path, yellow waymark), go through a kissing gate and a tunnel of rhododendrons and past a little summer-house. Clovelly Court stands impassively on the left surrounded by extensive grounds. Beyond a tall kissing gate at a deer fence and forking right, you join a track coming up from the left and reach Angel Wings, an extraordinary canopied seat of elaborate design. Put up in 1826, restored in 1934 and in memory of Marion Stuckley who loved Clovelly, the structure at the time of writing badly needs renovating before the elements wreck it. Carved in the wood are many interesting names and dates of past visitors.

Our onward route now forks right in woodland above the sheer cliff of Gallantry Bower, dropping steeply and turning left at a waymark post. From here a sharp turn right onto a stony track leads seawards to Mouth Mill. The more adventurous with time to spare could turn right at the waymark post and explore several sensational clifftop viewpoints, connected by paths and ending in a very steep, though not dangerous, descent to **MOUTH MILL**. (In wet and windy conditions or if unhappy with the gradient, simply retrace steps to pick up the official path.)

At Mouth Mill, the way keeps left of the sea wall, crosses the stream and goes left along by a derelict lime-kiln. Before leaving, however, a quick look at the pebbly beach is worthwhile, for just to the right rises Blackchurch Rock, an impressive arched structure offering some climbing routes.

Opposite a cottage over to the left, the coast path swings right, climbing steeply through woods to a stile and a National Trust sign for Brownsham. Much of the clifftop to Hartland Point is owned by the National Trust and their signs become familiar features.

The way continues on round a field, heading towards a sharp ridge of land ahead and passing a path left to Brownsham and Beckland. Recently made, the seaward path forms big zig-zags down to the next remote little valley to cross Beckland Water. Passing another path off left, keep right and soon there is an exciting retrospective view of Blackchurch Rock, from here a curious pyramid with 2 arches. Ever widening prospects greet you as the ridge-like crest is gained on Windbury Point. Clifftop walking leads on through a gate and forward along a field edge *(a footpath connects with the car park at Brownsham Farm).*

Next to negotiate is a smaller combe with wooden footbridge and steps up. Thereafter the walking becomes significantly easier - though for a while somewhat more monotonous - along flat field edges and past a National Trust Fattacott sign. Crossing a small stream in a thicket, the path winds in and out of indentations above sheer cliffs. The triangulation pillar behind Chapman Rock stands in a hedge but provides an exact positional check if an O.S. map is being used. Originally the coast path was to have veered inland here, but a combination of good sense, National Trust acquisitions, a helpful Ministry of Defence and encouragement from the South West Way Association yielded a truly coastal route in line with the spirit of the South West Way.

Beyond a small gorse-filled depression, Hartland Point buildings and the village church tower inland are in sight as you round Eldern Point (walk out from the path for the best panoramas). The route goes right round the back of Shipload Bay, held within steep scrubby cliffs. There is a new National Trust path down to East Titchberry beach - a rare stretch of sand between Westward Ho! and the Cornwall border. In 1884 the first undersea cable to Lundy Island was laid here but Atlantic seas swept it away and it was relocated.

The coast path emerges onto a broad track by a Devon Fund collection box and forks right at a bench and 'New Path to Beach' sign. *(East Titchberry car park straight on)*. The old path is closed owing to subsidence, but equally fine views back of dramatic cliff folding are obtained from the new one. Massive stone-faced and hedged banks up to 8ft. high which characterise field boundaries here are typically Devonian and date back many hundreds of years.

Skirting scenically outside the M.O.D. Radar Station's perimeter fence (all credit to the authorities for their cooperation), the path drops right to a very unscenic car park above Barley Bay: there is usually a refreshment hut nearby in the summer. Turn right along the lane past an old water catchment area and just before the lighthouse gates (once open to visits, the lighthouse is now automated), turn left up a concrete path, left again by the Coastguard enclosure and right at the clifftop. (The Coastguard Station is open to visits weekday afternoons but is due for closure.) There is an infrequent bus service from Hartland village to Clovelly and Bideford, though to reach it involves a 3½ mile (5.6km) tramp along country roads.

This is **HARTLAND POINT**, 325ft. (99m) high and one of the great turning points on the South West Way. Ahead, the coast increases in exposure and grandeur by the mile and there is precious little shelter from the prevailing westerlies and Atlantic swells until the Lizard has been rounded. 182 miles (293km) of glorious walking separates us here from that most southerly part of mainland Britain -walking which often is unsurpassed in quality anywhere in Europe, some would say the world.

The transition from predominantly north-facing coast to west-facing is immediately apparent. Cliffs and rock reefs are ravaged by the ocean's unremitting onslaught, now free from Lundy's breakwater effect: never was a shoreline more threatening to shipping. Wrecks litter the coast but are soon broken up and dispersed by wave action. Perhaps still visible just south of the lighthouse at the time of your visit will be the wreck of the Panamanian registered coaster 'Johanna'.

Hartland Point

Damehole Point

Both the walking and cliff architecture become more rugged in character as we turn south. Indeed, they are inextricably linked as extensive geological folding and erosion effects - some of the finest examples in Britain - have created successive switchbacks to sap the coastal traveller's energy! Yet the rewards for hard work are supreme and, given a modicum of good luck with the weather, the 45 miles (72km) of hiking from here to Port Isaac will be unforgettable.

The startling, cutaway profile of Damehole Point first commands attention as you skirt fields and drop into a small valley by Upright Cliff. Heading left past a static caravan, Titchberry Water is crossed on a substantial bridge and the climb out is steep at first before veering seaward. Damehole Point's loose, knife-edge arête is accessible by definitive right of way, a sensational scramble for those with a steady head and in quiet conditions. The coast path descends into Smoothlands Valley, the originl course of Titchberry Water and still prone to bogginess. (The old routing stays up left). In springtime, drifts of blue spring squill combine with the unusual topography to create a unique sense of beauty here.

After crossing the little stream you mount a crest of shaley rock up Blegberry Cliff (care needed in windy weather), giving a fantastic bird's-eye perspective over rock reefs and pounding surf. Once over Blegberry Water (detour right to see a spectacular waterfall), keep to the cliff edge, seaward of a house on the climb up; the path drops abruptly to grassy levels at Blackpool Mill. At the bottom, turn left, pass behind a white cottage and turn right over boggy ground, through a gate and along by the Abbey River, crossing it at a bridge and returning shorewards. Just over a mile upstream, the river flows by Hartland Abbey, founded in the 11th century and rebuilt as a private residence in 1860.

The best line now goes right to the coast below Dyer's Lookout and turns up left adjacent to the river mouth. Distractions on the climb are the lovely, slender 15th century tower of Stoke Church and the stark ruin of Warren Tower on the skyline ahead. Little is clear about the Tower's origins, though it seems likely to have begun as a lookout before being converted by the owners of Hartland Abbey into a summer-house.

At a small cottage (the erstwhile rocket apparatus house), turn right on a broad path, then off to the left just down the road if not intending to break your walk here. If rest or refreshment are sought, go downhill to **HARTLAND QUAY** (*hotel - accommodation and teas; Green Ranger bar - food; shop - confectionery and gifts, no groceries; museum and car park*). Severe gales at the end of the 19th century completely destroyed the once busy harbour and quay here.

SECTION 9 - Hartland Quay to Bude; 13 miles (21km)

This is undoubtedly one of the most testing stretches of path on the entire north coast and should be given due consideration before setting out. It is also unspoiled and scenically very rewarding. A couple of down-and-ups bring you to an outstanding beach waterfall, whereafter the clifftop is regained above a rocky shore renowned for its shipwrecks. A short walk on a country lane is followed by gorse and rough pasture and a steep drop to Welcombe Mouth. There now ensues a switchback of big ascents and descents as the path negotiates a succession of 5 deep combes. Marsland Mouth marks the border between Devon and Cornwall and there is a possible inland detour to Morwenstow for refreshment at about the half-way point.

More stiff gradients lead on past the aerial dishes of a government communications station, out to a precipitous headland and down to a road end at Duckpool. One climb later and the worst is over! Sandy and Northcott

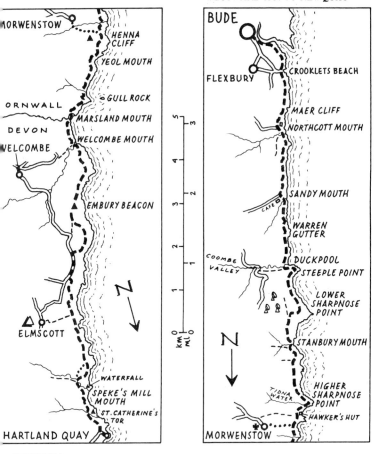

SECTION 9
HARTLAND QUAY to BUDE

Mouths both return walkers to civilision and gentle, grassy slopes lead effortlessly down to Bude.   Grading - strenuous.
Youth hostel at Elmscott, just off route. Inn, seasonal tea rooms and possible B&B at Morwenstow. National Trust cafe, toilets at Sandy Mouth. Seasonal refreshments at Northcott Mouth.

89

NOTE: Before departing from Hartland Quay it is advisable to take stock of the weather outlook, time of day and overnight accommodation arrangements (there is a youth hostel some 3 miles - 4.8km ahead). Also review food and spare clothing being carried and levels of fatigue. The next 13 miles (21km) are as rough and demanding as any on our official long-distance paths and are not for the fainthearted or for unfavourable circumstances, especially stormy weather. There is much up-and-down work, there are no bus services on the nearest roads and there is only one place of refreshment - Morwenstow at around half-way.

Having sounded a sensible warning, it should be added that this is also one of the most unspoiled, unfrequented and scenically stunning sections of coast open to public access and therefore one which the serious walker will not on any acount want to miss. Leaving an extra margin of time for the jourey will allow for rests and increase your enjoyment.

Walking back up the road, watch for a turning right, over a stile and into a Devon Trust Nature Reserve *(no camping)*, set up mainly to preserve the habitat of the Large Blue butterfly. The coast path drops grassily round the great cut-off rock ridge of St. Catherine's Tor, believed to have borne a 14th century chapel although no remains exist. Crossing Wargery Water on stepping stones, keep ahead to a wall then veer right up to a fence on the skyline.

The course of Wargery Water, like Titchberry Water and others, now ends more abruptly than it once did before the encroachment of sea erosion. There is in fact a waterfall, though the old beach path has largely slipped away. In the vicinity are many species of wildflowers – pink thrift, birdsfoot trefoil, foxglove and red campion, to name but a few.

A stiff 200ft. (61m) pull brings you over to **SPEKE'S MILL MOUTH** and one of the finest waterfalls on the entire south-west coast. Cascading 52ft. (16m) to the beach below, its full extent is not readily appreciated by peering over the bank. If you are a confident scrambler and neither stream level nor tide is high, it is possible by keeping well to the right to descend direct to the beach. Here go left to the stream's mouth and climb up to the left beside the series of falls, to emerge opposite the main cascade.

A motorable track reaches the valley and the coast path turns inland on this for 150m before branching down right over a footbridge. Angling back to the right, a coast path signpost is reached, whereafter make directly for the cliff crest ahead on Swansford Hill. (Until fairly recently the official path went up the valley behind and could still be

The waterfall at Speke's Mill Mouth

used in extremely windy weather.) Keep your eyes skinned, as the cliff edge appears suddenly in front of your feet! It is a truly fabulous situation with views across Speke's Mill Mouth valley back to St. Catherine's Tor, Hartland Quay and Damehole Point, and ahead to beyond Tintagel.

Walking along the edges of flat fields above 400ft. (122m) cliffs, spare a thought for seamen and ships which have been lost below - 136 in the last 200 years on this stretch of coast. Most recent to founder was the 'Green Ranger', a Royal Fleet Auxiliary tanker which parted her tow in a November gale in 1962 and was wrecked on the Longpeak rocks. Her crew of seven were rescued with considerable difficulty by breeches buoy after concerted efforts from Hartland coastguards, the Appledore lifeboat and a helicopter from RAF Chivenor. Rusty winching gear still lies strewn on the clifftop alongside the path.

At a small erosion diversion - the cliffs are crumbling away all along here - a path leaves left for Hartland youth hostel at Elmscott. For a while, the path ahead is inside the field fence before a left turn leads out to the road at a conspicuous white signpost. Go right along the tarmac for ½ mile (10 minutes) and watch out for a signed track on the right at the far end of a field containing radio masts above Sandhole Cliff. This takes you back to the cliff edge and past mysterious fenced-off installations which may or may not be permanent and whose purpose is obscure, to the author at least!

At first on a farm track, a mile of gentle ascent in wide and open surroundings reminiscent of moorland leads on to Embury Beacon, a gorse-scattered, sheepy promontory bearing the remains of an Iron Age camp. So rapidly are the cliffs falling away hereabouts that an emergency dig was initiated in 1973 to excavate the site before it was lost for good. Domestic pottery and timbers were found from the ancient dwelling huts and cattle enclosures. Today not much is left and in a few centuries all will have vanished into the hungry ocean.

Once past Knap Head, notorious for shipwrecks, the coast path turns down right. Dangerously steep at one time, the descent to Welcombe Mouth has been fitted with timber steps which may annoy purists but undeniably prevents further erosion from walkers picking their own lines down the slope.

Popular for its sands and picnic spots, **WELCOMBE MOUTH** is accessible to motor vehicles by dirt road from the village 1½ miles (2.4km) inland *(pub; possible supplies from nearby farm)*. The Victorian eccentric the Rev. R.S.Hawker, of whom more later, was incumbent of this parish and Morwenstow in the mid-1800's.

Crossing Strawberry Water on the concrete stepping stones, loins will need girding up for the ensuing gradients which follow in relentless succession through five big combes - potentially hard going with a heavy pack. First heading right on a stony track, climbing begins in earnest up to a hilltop field with two massive railway-sleeper stiles. The descent to Marsland Mouth is a steep one and passes an audaciously positioned stone cabin, once belonging to the poet-playwright Ronald Duncan.

Zig-zags lead down and Charles Kingsley's description of this coast in *Westward Ho!* never seemed more apt: '...To landward all richness, softness and peace; to seaward, a waste and howling wilderness of rock and roller, barren to the fisherman and hopeless to the shipwrecked mariner...'

The little footbridge over **MARSLAND WATER** downstream from its miniature gorge marks the coastal boundary between North Devon and Cornwall. Remote and grand in scale, the Cornish coast beckons with both a foretaste of the splendours to come and a contrast to the busier resort areas encountered farther south.

Over the stream the way follows a good track inland for 200m then turns off sharply back right at a sign and up Marsland Cliff. From its level top, note the amazing folded arch of Gull Rock running offshore. Almost immediately you are losing height again down a long series of

Marsland Mouth - Devon's lonely border with Cornwall

timber steps into the next big combe. At the bottom, keep left by a fence then go right over the footbridge above Little Water, which ends in a 70ft. (21m) waterfall. Already there are fewer concessions to human passage than on more populous stretches of the South West Way: bridges are simply double telegraph poles which call for steady footwork in windy conditions.

Cornakey Cliff is the next obstacle - a hefty pull up to 400ft. (122m). Field undulations follow to another stile: are they extra tall to deter nimble sheep?! The coast path goes downhill by a cliff edge fence and crosses Yeol Water at its seaward end, thereafter climbing to a post on Henna Cliff. At 450ft. (137m), this is the English coast's 2nd highest sheer cliff after Beachy Head and views are correspondingly wider than ever, taking in Morwenstow Church to the left and the aerial dishes on the Composite Signals Organisation Station. Looking back, the Devon coast is visible as far as Damehole Point, the truncated profile of St. Catherine's Tor and even the buildings of Hartland Quay.

Before the big descent to Morwenstow Water, there is an opportunity to break the walk and visit **MORWENSTOW** itself *(seasonal tea rooms just above the churchyard; the Bush Inn opposite the green; local farms sometimes offer B&B)*. To reach the hamlet stay on the inland path, returning to the coast on the far side of the combe at Vicarage

Cliff.

The writer and reverend extraordinaire R.S.Hawker, Morwenstow's parish priest in the mid-19th century, is best known for his 'Song of the Western Men' (though not in his own lifetime) and for instituting the celebration of Harvest Festival. Many unfortunate shipwreck victims are buried in the churchyard, where you can also see the wooden figurehead of the Scottish brig 'Caledonia', wrecked more than 140 years ago. The Rectory chimneys are said to resemble the church towers from Hawker's previous incumbencies.

500m or so will bring you back above the shoreline on Vicarage Cliff but if the diversion to Morwenstow has not been made, simply cross Morwenstow Water at its seaward end and from the National Trust sign climb onto Vicarage Cliff. **HAWKER'S HUT** is only 10m down from the clifftop. Here in his driftwood cabin, the eccentric parson used to sit smoking opium and write in solitude, though he was visited on occasions by both Tennyson and Kingsley in the 1840's. The structure is now in the hands of the National Trust.

Down again, the coast path traverses the valley of Tidna Water and rises steeply to an old wartime lookout. Seaward from here lies an exhilarating little detour out on **HIGHER SHARPNOSE POINT,** though not recommended in wind. The narrow spur - virtually an arête - gives airy views of unsurpassed quality and will itself be in sight as a prominent feature for a long way south.

There is a small valley running behind if a gale is blowing, otherwise the way continues up ruggedly to the lofty clifftop and follows field edges. Here and there old stiles, once on the path, have slipped away 20 or 30 metres below, witness to persistent erosion by the sea.

The tracking station ahead now appears close at hand but is separated from you by one of the least friendly combes on this switchback. Stanbury Water has to be crossed near its mouth where there is an awkward little ravine. Quite a lot of concreting has been done to consolidate the path here, which continues down to the pebbly beach. *(If needed, there is a telephone at the first farm up the lane.)* Another minimal footbridge takes you over the stream where you turn up steps and engage the slope ahead, back to the 400ft. (122m) contour.

At the top, the path aims for a corner in the tracking station fence, passes a bench and reaches a stile. Now simply walk along the metalled access road for 100m and turn right, back to the clifftop. Visible from afar in both directions, the enormous aerial dishes belong to the Composite Signals Organisation Station (once RAF Cleave) and temporarily drag one back to a technological society. In reality an outpost of G.C.H.Q., the station monitors Soviet satellites and probably

Higher Sharpnose Point

much else besides. Ominous or beautiful, depending on personal inclination, the structures are impressive reminders of the age in which we live.

There are rock climbs on Lower Sharpnose Point, as on many other Cornish sea cliffs. The coast path soon passes a National Trust 'Duckpool' sign and at a cairned post goes seaward towards Steeple Point. Be sure to continue to the end of the point under its sharp crest - the path is well made and eventually angles back down inland to **DUCKPOOL** *(car park, toilets)*.

Not until 1981, 8 years after the official opening of the South West Way, was a bridge constructed over the river here in green Combe Valley. Until then, walkers encountered problems in time of spate or storm when the river mouth boulder crossing - normally quite safe - was impassable. The Forestry Commission has laid out a Nature Trail on the south side of Combe Valley.

50m beyond the public toilets near the road end, turn right over a stile, cross the bridge and turn right up the cliffs to Warren Gutter. Descending over a boggy depression, yet another hard climb is required to reach Stowe Cliffs. Walkers who have come from Hartland Quay will be encouraged to learn that the stiffest gradients are now behind and that the way ahead to Bude is but an undulating stroll. Walkers going north, however, have it all to do until reaching Knap Head.

The route drops to cross a small stream; adjacent cliff edges are like grassy cornices, to be treated with a similar respect to that which their snowy cousins enjoy! Soon a track leads down to **SANDY MOUTH** *(National Trust seasonal cafe; car park; toilets)*.

A stile points the way forward onto lower cliffs, along past numerous landslips ploughed thoughtlessly to the edge at times. (For students of geology, an alterntive routing lies along the beach, but the tide should be low or on the ebb to avoid being caught out: escape is possible at Northcott Mouth.) Pass a conspicuous Bronze Age barrow near Menachurch Point and drop down steps to **NORTHCOTT MOUTH** *(seasonal refreshments)*. Concrete wartime tank-traps are still in evidence, but there is a fine low-tide, sandy beach along which it is only a mile to Bude.

Cross the track and keep ahead up the grassy slope. Owing to serious land slippage, the coast path is diverted inland of a bungalow on a broad track, returning to the cliff edge after passing through a gate. With Poughill church now in view, it is all gently downhill over short cropped turf to the first buildings of Bude; a stile and path lead to Crooklets Beach.

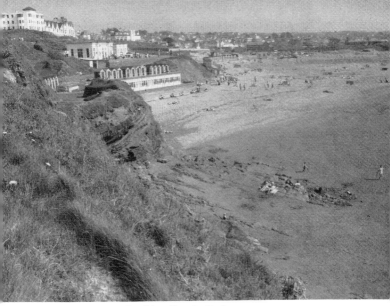

Crooklets Beach, Bude

It is hard to imagine, but after a severe storm in 1936, the beach was left entirely devoid of sand from the scouring action of huge waves. Britain's first Surf Lifesaving Club was founded here in 1953 and the boisterous ocean is popular with belly-boarding holidaymakers and malibu-board experts alike. Bude was once dubbed the 'Second Bondi'!

There is no shortage of refreshment places, but **BUDE** itself *(all shops, services and accommodation; Tourist Office; campsites; bus routes to Taunton and Exeter for BR main line connections; early closing Thursday.)* unusually stands back from the coast so that its rows of hotels and its hilly shopping streets are largely unseen at first.

Although lacking the charm of more picturesque resorts on the South West Way, Bude and nearby Stratton are bustling with visitors during the summer and represent a return to civilisation for the south-bound walker. Adjacent roads boast bus services - an increasingly rare commodity in the rural south-west - and there are direct links with the main rail network at Taunton and Exeter, enabling walkers to start or finish a stage here.

From Crooklets Beach, turn right past snack bars, and continue along the seafront 'promenade'. Above Summer Leaze Beach you pass

Sea lock-gates, Bude Canal

the cricket ground and a topographic viewing pillar with flagpole (not O.S. but a donated monument) before swinging inland. At low tide it is possible to cross the River Neet's mouth.

A little upstream, the river is crossed by a larger footbridge: follow Tourist Information signs past Bude Castle (Council Offices) and walk along the canal quayside. The Local History Museum is well worth visiting.

Canals are not a common feature of the Cornish coast and Bude's is even more unusual. Engineered by a James Green and opened after long delays in 1823, it worked on the principle of wheeled barges being hauled up inclined ramps as an alternative to conventional locks. The technology was well ahead of its time and ultimately proved unreliable, the canal closing around the end of the century.

SECTION 10 - Bude to Boscastle;   16 miles (26km)

A strenuous day! Grassy clifftops and another popular bay to begin with precede a minor combe and fields above landslipped cliffs and a climb to the Dizzard, highest point so far in Cornwall. A very long and steep descent to

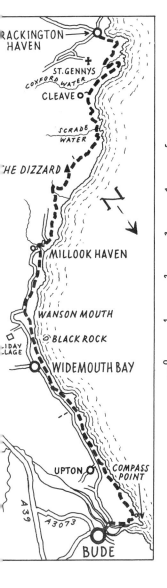

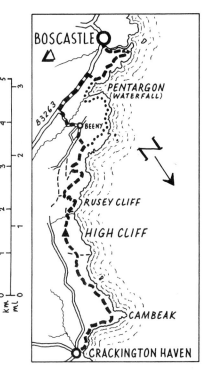

**SECTION 10
BUDE to BOSCASTLE**

cross a stream valley and a stiff pull up lead you on to exciting, undulating sea edge walking, but care is needed due to erosion along the clifftop. Dramatic rock formations flank Crackington Haven and the onward path. High Cliff is true to its name but the ascent is gradual, followed by another steep and rugged drop over a combe. Further high quality walking brings you to Pentargon waterfall (the eroded path is reinstated) and round rocky outcrops to Boscastle's inlet harbour. Grading - easy at first then more difficult.

Refreshments, supplies and accommodation at Widemouth Bay, including campsite; also toilets. Refreshments, accommodation and campsite at Crackington Haven.

Walk left over the sea-lock gates, past the old lifeboat house (Bude now has an Inshore Rescue Boat), up steps and turn right onto the coast path proper. (If desired, continue ahead onto the breakwater. The original structure was destroyed by a storm in 1838 and even now Bude Haven is hardly the most friendly place for boats, with its narrow channel and relentless surf.)

Steps lead left up onto Efford Down and past the tower with compass points on octagonal facets. It is a wonderful viewpoint over Bude and Stratton, back to the aerial dishes of Composite Signals Organisation Station, inland to the Dartmoor tors and ahead - perhaps as far as the distant profiles of Tintagel Hotel and Trevose Head 30 miles (48km) distant.

You follow a line of posts back from the crumbling cliff edge, keeping left through a wall gate. Passing a topographic pillar, go through a newish stile in the middle of the wall ahead then veer back seaward and up to the next stile.

For a while now, path quality takes a nosedive, first flanking houses by a fence then turning right on a roadside path at Upton. Untidy development crowds in on the coastal walker, though there is compensation in the form of tea-rooms at a Widemouth Bay road sign. Down and up to a bungalow and there is a view ahead over Widemouth Bay - another popular beach and surfing venue, but suffering from over-use and consequent lack of consideration for the adjacent environment.

Descend to a car park and on behind a cottage and outbuildings (the path was once to seaward). Turn left to the road at an Off Licence/ Store and along it for 50m, then right down across a car park *(seasonal refreshments; toilets)*. Beyond **WIDEMOUTH BAY** *(Post Office; pub; shop; accommodation; campsite; early closing Wednesday)* there are no sleeping or eating places until Crackington Haven, some 7 miles

(11km) ahead; the walking also gets considerably tougher!

By either taking to the sands or staying on the duney foreshore, the prominent Black Rock is approached, whereafter the coast path climbs onto cliffs, veers left up a track and along through undergrowth, before turning right onto the country road. Here at Wanson Mouth there is serious erosion and even the road is subsiding!

After a lay-by, the path turns right alongside the road, then follows field edges above Penhalt Cliff, soon dropping to Millook Haven. This is reminiscent of Devon combes, though not the contorted rock strata on the cove's northern side (best seen on the climb out) which are extraordinary enough to be textbook examples. In 1835, plans were put forward to construct a small port here but the project never materialised.

Descend to the hamlet and road hairpin above Millook's pebbly beach, then climb the steep road hill (possible short-cut of bend). Before the top, turn right over a waymarked stile, as the path continues along clifftops between thorn bushes.

The land has slipped badly hereabouts and you make for a waymark post along the edge of a large field above scrubby cliff-falls. As the way heads inland a little to cross a stream in charming woodland of sessile oak, you are increasingly likely to see heather and wild roses, sea-pinks and even purple-spotted orchids near the path. Climbing out the woods and round field edges, you are above extensive landslipped and overgrown cliffs.

Keep right of a wired enclosure, cross a stile behind it and the O.S. triangulation pillar on the **DIZZARD** is reached - at 538ft. (164m) the highest point so far in Cornwall. Retrospective views take in Higher Sharpnose Point, while the distinctive profile of Cambeak draws attention ahead.

From the Dizzard, keep right over a stile (not the gate ahead) and along above low woods of sessile oak and blackthorn, ignoring steps up to the left. The way crosses two streamlets and climbs back above more low woodland.

At Chipman Point starts an exceptionally long and steep descent to cross Scrade Water which falls to the beach in a double waterfall from its deep, V-shaped valley. Once over the footbridge, the bank is in danger of collapsing at the time of writing and the subsequent hard pull up would benefit from zig-zags. In wet weather, the laden walker will not find this comfortable! At the top, stay round the cliff edge, go over a stile and down across a smaller stream valley, with 11th century St. Gennys church on the hillside ahead. A sequence of clifftop stiles leads on to where you drop round through gorse and head excitingly

The coast between Crackington Haven and Boscastle

seaward along a ridge.

A National Trust sign announces this as 'Cleave; given in memory of Bob and Joan Wilton of Kenya and Aldbrough St. John Yorkshire'. The path becomes precariously eroded and will need regular re-routing as the land is eaten away. The author almost met his Maker here when, after a spell of unusually wet weather followed by a rapidly drying strong wind, a 2-metre section of cliff immediately in front of his feet simply slid from view like a descending lift, taking the path with it. It was a salutory experience but not one which could have been anticipated.

You come down through heather and swing inland alongside Coxford Water. The sea is cutting back the valley mouth and its north wall simultaneously and will eventually force the stream to divert its course, much as has occurred elsewhere on this coast. Cross the foot-bridge and climb to a post on the skyline, turning right by a fence then doubling back round the cliff edge.

After contouring above a cove at Pencannow Point (worth detouring to for views), fork left up to a stile, go along right by the fence then angle left all the way down to **CRACKINGTON HAVEN** *(hotel; inn; restaurants; accommodation; campsite; cafe; beach shop; toilets; telephone; car park; early closing Thursday)*. The best since Widemouth Bay, Crackington's sands are dominated by 400ft. (122m) cliffs of contorted strata. Once a port exporting slate and importing coal and lime (boats just ran onto the beach at high tide), Crackington Haven has opened itself to a modest degree of tourism and is certainly a welcome punctuation mark for walkers on this fine stretch of unin-habited coast.

Another 7 miles (12km) of strenuous hiking over Cornwall's highest cliff separate us from the next refreshments and accommodation at Boscastle. Before leaving Crackington Haven, those with time to spare could walk up the Coxford road and in about 800m turn left to St. Gennys church, dedicated to St. Genesius who, the story goes, carried his head around after being decapitated! A path goes due west to Pencannow Point for a return on the coast path.

The way now leaves from the south side of Crackington beach, past a tennis court and National Trust pillar: most of the ensuing 3 miles (4.8km) represents a gift in memory of aircrew lost during the Battle of Britain. Beyond a high wooden fence, open cliffs are reached again, overgrown below with scrubby woodland. In 1836 Tremoutha Haven was designated by Act of Parliament to become a harbour and resort named Port Victoria, served by a railway link with Launceston. However, like Millook Haven near Widemouth Bay, actual development never got off the ground.

Rock strata continue to impress as two deep little stream valleys and a cattle-churned depression lead you out towards Cambeak. In quiet weather and with great discretion, the surefooted can keep forward onto the narrow headland summit itself - 'a gruesome place, so narrow its head, so sheer the precipice'. The normal path doubles back left and in very windy conditions you could use the small valley behind the point.

There are remains of a quay below, though ships would have needed benign seas to use it. When opposite threatening Samphire Rock, look back for the best prospect of Northern Door rock arch but beware the crumbling edge from now on to High Cliff.

Crossing an electric fence, you meet a well maintained path leading from a car park to the beach but you soon fork left at a waymark post to traverse a boggy area in a steep little valley, with large-scale land-slippage to the right. The final climb to **HIGH CLIFF** (732ft. - 223m) is a good deal easier than many a previous one; there is also access from the nearby coastal by-road. Both Boscastle and the square profile of Tintagel Hotel are visible ahead. Despite lacking a sheer seaward drop, this loftiest point on the Cornwall coast path is dramatic enough and can be inhospitable indeed during a gale or dense sea mist.

Another hazardous descent, and a big one at that, hugs the steep, unstable cliff edge. Over the stream, it is important to locate the correct routing up landslipped Rusey Cliff and to avoid arriving at either the beach or road. When the path ahead (the middle one of three when seen from High Cliff) snakes on downhill, branch up left. At a large hollow the way swings left again, whereafter follow the main zig-zags back and right to the clifftop (road access).

One up-and-down later you will round Buckator headland, to be confronted by a green and marshy V-shaped valley. It is tempting (and many try, including the author!) to take one of the thin trods straight across, but the ground is extremely wet and there is barbed wire to negotiate. The correct line detours round inland to pass some large white boulders. Gull Rock is backed by dark, vertical rock walls.

A few stiles farther on stands a notice warning 'Cliffs dangerous at Pentargon'. The original coast path kept to Beeny Cliff over Fire Beacon Point and above grey seals' breeding ground at Seals Hole. The splendid 120ft. (36m) waterfall at Pentargon was seen to good advantage. Cliff-falls, however, necessitated re-routing on a 1½ mile (2.4km) diversion inland to a busy main road without verges. At the time of writing it is understood that Cornwall County Council are about to open a new, safe path close to the old one, thus happily obvi-

Pentargon Waterfall (left)

ating a road walk probably more dangerous to life and limb during the busy summer season than the eroding cliffs themselves!

The road diversion, if still in force, ends at a kissing gate on the right and regains the cliffs along to Penally Hill with its flagpole. Penally Point offers the best views and you then walk down past rocky outcrops to **BOSCASTLE** *(most shops, services and accommodation; youth hostel; pubs; National Trust Information Centre and shop; toilets; telephone; car park; early closing Thursday)*.

North of Padstow there are few natural havens for shipping other than Bude and Port Isaac. Boscastle is the exception and for several centuries after Sir Richard Grenville built its inner jetty during Elizabeth I's reign, it was a thriving port. Picturesque though it undeniably is, this tortuous channel at the mouth of the River Valency, with its perilously narrow entrance between black cliffs, would have been nightmarish to negotiate under sail. Ships were often towed in by 'hobblers' - boats with eight oarsmen - and further steered by men on shore with ropes. That the port was commercially active for so long bears witness to the scarcity of shelter on this exposed coast and the lack of a rail link until 1893 when Camelford Station opened.

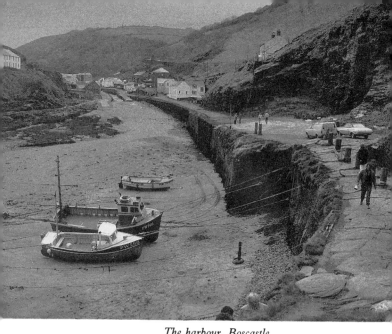

The harbour, Boscastle

Boscastle derives its name from the French de Bottreaux family whose manor house or 'castle' has long since disappeared. The National Trust owns most of the immediate area and has a shop and Information Centre on the quay near the youth hostel. It is a pretty village whose steep street is lined with thatched cottages and which receives large numbers of tourists during the summer. All this frenetic activity might well bemuse the coastal walker accustomed to many miles of untouched cliff with only seabirds and the voice of the sea as company. However, the amenities will doubtless be welcome and the upper village is much quieter - well worth exploring if time allows.

SECTION 11 - Boscastle to Port Isaac;   13 miles (21km)

Fascinating and high quality walking to Tintagel, with its famous island castle and very busy in the season. Easy going at first past old slate quarries, but beyond Trebarwith Strand an exceptionally strenuous 6 miles (10km) to Port Isaac as the path negotiates a long series of remote combes with one or two fierce gradients to contend with. Despite this and some cliff edge erosion, a magnificent stretch of wild, rough walking.   Grading - moderate

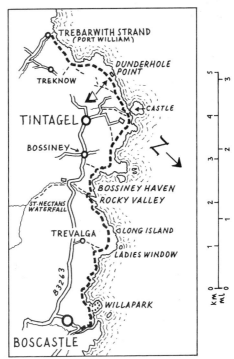

SECTION 11
BOSCASTLE to TREBARWITH STRAND

then strenuous.
All shops, services and accommodation, including youth hostel, at Tintagel.
Hotel, seasonal restaurant and pub at Trebarwith Strand. Accommodation
and refreshments at Port Gaverne, just before Port Isaac.

Cross the River Valency, walk along Boscastle's quayside and climb
the rocky path onto cliffs, with more superb views. For sheer quality
combined with accessibility, the stretch to Tintagel is highly recommended as an easy 5 mile (8km) day walk which really shouldn't be
rushed. Boscastle's outer jetty was constructed towards the end of the
18th century but had to be rebuilt by the National Trust in 1962,
having been severely damaged by a mine during the Second World
War. Stone from Plymouth's old Laira Bridge was used, and to aid

107

'Curzyway' wall and stile

access a light railway was laid along the north side of the harbour.

Willapark headland's white tower was a customs lookout in days when smugglers and the Revenue men were constantly endeavouring to outwit each other. You can go right out onto Cliff Castle, a promontory fort. Inland is a good example of strip cultivation, a relatively uncommon sight in this age of mechanised farming which has obliterated so many signs of our agricultural history; even this one is vulnerable to the plough.

Keep to the cliff edge as the path undulates, dropping over Grower Gut and climbing again past slate waste, over a stile up a bank, with duckboarding on a marshy section. The stone stile ahead is in a wall of herringbone formation known as 'curzyway' and characteristic of the region. With Trevalga church tower and manor house on the cliff ahead, you walk onto a rutted farm track. Before the gate, turn right and contour round; views extend back to High Cliff and beyond, forward to Tintagel's prominent headland hotel, now appreciably closer.

Soon, on Firebeacon Hill, you will see Ladies Window, a remarkable rock aperture and shortly afterwards the sensational 200ft. (61m) vertical stack of Long Island, topped by a rock climbers' cairn. The entertaining path continues past a campsite and veers inland into

Rocky Valley.

Turning seaward, you cross a stream tumbling dramatically between jagged rock outcrops to the sea. **ROCKY VALLEY** is best known for its Bronze Age 'maze' carvings. (These and other interesting diversions, including a tea-room at Trevillet Mill and St. Nectan's waterfall beyond the B3263 road, are found by detouring up the luxuriantly wooded footpath alongside the stream. Allow an hour to reach the waterfall and return.)

Steps lead up from Rocky Valley - once used by donkeys - to a post and bench, whereafter the coast path continues round above Bossiney Haven. Legend has it that King Arthur's round table is buried in an ancient earthworks to the west of Bossiney village.

You are invited to 'call in for cream teas, lunches, snacks etc.' at Willa Park Hotel just off-route to the left. Such wayside temptations testify to the popularity of the path near Tintagel, associated as it is with the mythical King Arthur, and a consequent tourist destination. Stone steps lead down to the Bossiney Haven beach path which you cross, climbing ahead by a cliff-rescue rope box. *(Car park and telephone up left.)* More steps bring you to the stream footbridge and a rocky ascent back to the clifftops, where there is a fine view of Lye Rock's amazing cut-away profile.

The next rise is another Willapark, like its predecessor at Boscastle an Iron Age fort and out onto which is a short detour. With the huge monolithic block of Tintagel Hotel now close at hand, the way skirts a wall then keeps well down right towards the famous Castle area itself, passing a National Trust sign for Barras Nose. Going round below the hotel, the Castle ramparts appear ahead and you drop into Castle Cove *(Hugh's Beach Cafe; toilets).*

The legend of King Arthur has only the most tenuous links with real historical evidence. Almost certainly a leader in the Celtic or post-Roman eras, Arthur's depiction as a medieval knight is attributable more to subsequent romantic distortion than fact. Even Tintagel itself seems an unlikely location for such a figure to have chosen in those distant times. Its original name of Trevena was changed to identify the place with Tennyson's 'Idylls of the King' and the revival of chivalry instigated by the writings of Sir Walter Scott.

The river drops as a waterfall to the sea and is crossed by the path which then turns up left on a broad track towards **TINTAGEL** *(all shops, services and accommodation; youth hostel ahead by the path; Tourist Information; toilets; car parks; buses; early closing Thursday).*

The coast path does not visit the village but walkers may wish to make the kilometre or so detour. Apart from the Old Post Office in a

The old post office, Tintagel

Tintagel Castle above Castle Cove

curious medieval manor house now owned by the National Trust, there is little to recommend the place, unless you are partial to the busy crush of motor-borne tourists and the bombardment of souvenir 'kitsch'.

During the peak season and on Public Holidays, the island Castle too is uncomfortably overrun and much of its romance lost. A 4-wheel drive shuttle service operates from the village, adding to those visitors who reach the Castle on foot. That said, it is well worth an hour or two's exploration if you have the time and the entrance kiosk is to the right in Castle Cove.

Built over a 3rd century Celtic monastery, the 12th century Castle was put up by Reginald de Cornwall, illegitimate son of Henry I, and extended in the 1300's by the Black Prince. It was, ignominiously, to become a prison and was ruinous by the 16th century, only fragments of the original structure remaining today. Even so, they are impressive enough, the inner and outer wards now separated by the ravages of marine erosion though once connected by drawbridge.

To proceed ahead, walk up the main track and fork off right at a sign for St. Materiana's church, an interesting Norman building on an exposed clifftop site just off the path. Zig-zags lead up by a wall and over a stone stile, whereafter a wide track is taken over much-used land close to Tintagel. You soon leave the crowds and vehicles behind. Where the track bends left, turn down right past Tintagel's youth hostel, adapted from Long Grass slate quarry offices on Dunderhole Point and surely one of the most spectacular hostel locations in the UK.

Contouring on grassy cliffs, Gull Rock appears like a shark's fin out in the bay. The path turns left up shaley slopes towards houses, with disused slate quarries below which were still in operation until around the 1930's. An incredible rock pinnacle was deliberately left by the quarrymen behind Hole Beach - some say as a shelter though more likely perhaps as of inferior quality. Ships were loaded by whim driven by a blindfolded donkey above Penhallic Point, while quarrymen were often lowered on ropes to work the slate beds.

You pass a cliff-rescue rope box and soon descend to **TREBAR-WITH STRAND** *(hotel; seasonal restaurant and pub; toilets)*. As Port William, this precarious little anchorage shipped locally blasted slate, though not without considerable risk to the ketches, and their crews. Trade was mainly with Appledore and Bideford and included coal and lime.

NOTE: Before leaving here, a word of caution! The 6 miles (10km) or so to Port Isaac are exceptionally strenuous. A long series of combes

111

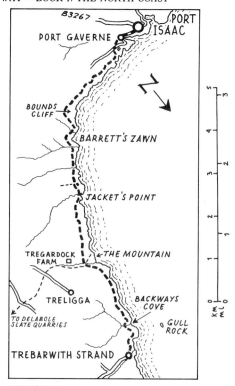

SECTION 11
TREBARWITH STRAND to PORT ISAAC

running to the sea creates steep gradients and the section rivals Hartland Quay to Bude for toughness, though only half the distance. It is also quite remote with no road access at all. You are advised to allow plenty of time and to carry some food and drink with you.

Walk up left towards the seasonal Port William pub then double back to the right of a white house. A long flight of steps leads up to a waymark post and along by a fence to the next post. At Dennis Point - 304ft. (93m) above sea level - the way veers back inland on any of several vague trods: aim for the post and footbridge over the stream which issues into lonely Backways Cove.

The first of a sequence of stiff ascents now awaits you, angling sea-

Quarry pinnacle behind Hole Beach; Gull Rock offshore

wards to the cliff edge on Start Point before verring back up left to the post above and a couple of Bronze Age burial mounds. Walking is now on rough, gorsey clifftop with fine views, including Port Isaac - our immediate destination. Going along by a field fence, the path is given little space but you soon swing inland towards Tregardock Farm.

'The Mountain' on maps proves innocuous enough - just a boggy little combe with an access path from the farm (and the B3314) to Tregardock Beach, which is non-existent at high tide! Cross over this path, but if there is time to spare turn up left to visit the famous Delabole Slate Quarries - open to visitors during the summer and about 2 miles (3km) each way.

The next climb is followed by skirting a thorn hedge and some delightful level walking. However, at the time of writing a red sign appears ahead - 'Caution Cliff Path cracked - use with extra care'. You could hop over into the field for extra safety, returning farther along over the wire fence: being aware of such dangers is part and parcel of being 'coastwise' and there is no virtue whatever in taking unnecessary risks!

After another precarious section close to the cliff edge, the path goes out to Jacket's Point then angles back down to a wooden footbridge (well waymarked). In very windy conditions go straight down very steeply by the fence and even more steeply up the other side - arguably the fiercest gradient on the entire South West Way! The newer routing climbs the cliff edge and at the top of steps goes right, following a field fence past a disused Coastguard Lookout (possible shelter) and down over a stile into the next combe. Cross the stream and angle right, then left up to the top.

The switchback continues - the next stream crossed is rather boggy. At the summit of the climb out, you are likely to encounter subsidence: this is another area of substanial landslippage and it is best to use a developing trod well back from the edge.

A very steep and often muddy descent by an old fence leads down to Barrett's Zawn ('zawn' means chasm). As you cross the stream at its seaward end, note a tunnel down to the right, once used by donkeys bringing out slate from the beach quarry below.

There now follows a long, sheepy ascent back inland (not as marked on most maps), the ground often churned up by hooves. However, from the top of lofty Bounds Cliff there are marvellous retrospective views along this spectacular coast. Keep to the field edges, up and on over stone stiles, watching for one down in a bottom field corner. Thorn hedges lead on and you drop into a little combe (beneath an unsightly rubbish tip at the time of writing). Duckboarding assists over the boggy stream, as do steps beyond. Passing old building rubble, there will be a growing impulse in most walkers to reach civilisation again and take a well earned breather. The buildings of Port Gaverne beckon and the route makes a beeline for them on a track to the road where you turn right, then left just before the Headlands Hotel. A steep, narrow lane between buildings brings you down to **PORT GAVERNE** *(hotel/pub/restaurant; beach cafe)*. If in a leisurely mood, a better approach to Port Gaverne eschews this direct line for a scenic walk round the last headland.

Charming and picturesque today, Port Gaverne was a busy little port for over two centuries, exporting from its jetty a vast tonnage of Delabole slate. The industry grew from the 1500's onwards and only declined when shipping became uneconomical and other cheaper materials began to supercede the labour-intensive, fragile slate. Port Gaverne was also a fishing community and although not as yet open to visits, the National Trust has acquired an old fish cellar for posterity.

There is a short road bash up to the one-time fishing village of **PORT ISAAC** *(all shops, services and accommodation; (restricted bank opening); Heritage Coast Information Centre in Old School Hotel, tel. Bodmin 880721; toilets; car parks; infrequent buses to Wadebridge; early*

Port Isaac

closing Wednesday).

Turn right through a car park at the top of the hill (waymarked), along a clifftop walk past guesthouses and down·through the village. Streets are narrow but the shops varied, offering interest and the chance to obtain supplies or refreshments. The harbour beach car park is at low tide only!

SECTION 12 - Port Isaac to Padstow;   10 miles (16km)

Once out above Port Isaac, 2½ miles (4km) of recently opened and out-standing cliff path undulating ruggedly to tiny Port Quin. Easy walking past coves out to Pentire Point, a majestic headland overlooking the Camel estuary and one of the South West Way's premier panoramic viewpoints. Pleasant slopes lead downhill to the surfing resort of Polzeath, followed by level going along the sandy estuary shores to Rock and the ferry for Padstow.   Grading - more difficult, then moderate to easy.

Shops, services and accommodation at Polzeath, also campsites. Refresh-ments and toilets at Daymer Bay.

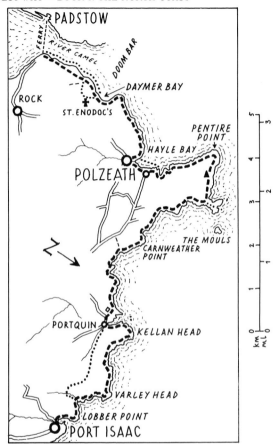

**SECTION 12
PORT ISAAC to PADSTOW**

Walk up the lane west of the quay and turn right, climbing to superlative views back over Port Isaac's pretty harbour. Once up round Lobber Point, the way drops to cross a stream above rocky Pine Haven. Until fairly recently, there was an inland stretch from here to Port Quin, but 2½ miles (4km) of completely new path has been cut at great expense close to the sea's edge - more exciting even than the

*Looking back to Kellan Head
from Trevan Point*

original Coastguard's path.

A steep pull up heralds many undulations, twists and turns. The way is clear but quite strenuous and only marred by an extravagantly high wooden fence topped by wire as if guarding some militarily sensitive frontier rather than marking the perimeter of farmland for the occasional hiker! Nevertheless, no walker will be disappointed by this entertaining section of path with its sudden corners and magnificent cliff views round Scarnor Point and Kellan Head.

There is a small car park at tiny **PORT QUIN** and the possibility, though not the guarantee, of teas during the summer season. Its row of holiday cottages was once a building for salting fish. After crossing the stream, walk up the lane and in 100m turn sharp right through a gateway to the National Trust's 'Doyden' property. Approaching the house, turn down right over grassy slopes to cross the main track at a stone pillar. Keep ahead towards fenced-off subsidence (antimony mines were sunk hereabouts); the castle-like folly up to the right was built around 1830 and is now a National Trust holiday let.

Rising gently, the way reaches a sign for Trevan Point - a high, rocky viewpoint - then drops to Lundy Bay. Threading behind the cove, you climb through the ubiquitous gorse which flowers on this coast for much of the year, in a lovely sheltered valley near stands of conifers. Stay seaward at a path fork (short-cut left to Polzeath, bypassing Pentire Point) and keep an eye open on the right for Lundy Hole, an extraordinary funnel depression protected by a wooden railing.

From Carnweather Point, the tower on Stepper Point is seen beyond sprawling Polzeath and the River Camel; even farther afield is Trevose Head. More legwork up over Cam Head is rewarded by good views, especially ahead to The Mouls, a sizeable rock island inhabited by seabirds, including puffins. Off route but a worthwhile detour, the Iron Age promontory fort on Rumps Point is better defined than many, its defensive earthworks clear to see across the intervening neck of land. Excavations in the 1960's unearthed 2,000 year-old pottery.

Cliff scenery is majestic on this most rugged headland and a little farther on lies **PENTIRE POINT** itself which, at 257ft. (79m) above the Camel estuary, provides probably the finest all round panorama on the whole South West Way. Its rocks contain notable examples of pillow lava.

An ambling path takes you pleasantly downhill towards Hayle Bay, passing behind Pentireglaze Haven and turning up right into the road through New Polzeath, a residential area with no amenities for the walker. A lane soon leads out to the seafront at **POLZEATH** (shops, services and accommodation; pub; cafe; campsites; toilets; car park; early closing Wednesday).

The ensuing section of path is easy and its quality improves after an indifferent start at Polzeath. This resort is very popular, however, and has a magnificent, safe sandy beach with good surf from the prevailing westerly fetch. If the tide is low, aim straight across the beach for the cafe; otherwise follow the road round over the bridge and at the start of the hill, look out for a waymarked turn off right between buildings. You are soon back out on the coast along The Greenaway, a broad swath of short-cropped turf round the southern side of Hayle Bay, with Stepper Point day mark tower conspicuous ahead. The Greenaway is less attractive in high season when it becomes a car park.

Winding along above low cliffs and below some delightfully situated properties, the coast path reaches Trebetherick Point, adjacent to the infamous **DOOM BAR**. These extensive mid-channel sands are the result of easterly currents funnelling material into the Camel estuary through the unique topography of its portal headlands. A navigable channel is maintained by dredging but is only usable by relatively

Pentire Point from The Greenaway, Polzeath

small vessels. Even in calm weather, the restless Atlantic swells rear up impressively as they encounter the sandbanks. In times of storm or heavy surge, Doom bar is an awesome sight and a severe threat to shipping, having claimed some 300 craft, including 3 lifeboats.

Coming round to **DAYMER BAY** *(cafe/beach shop; car park; toilets).* there are several possible routings ahead before catching the ferry to Padstow. At low water, simply walk along the sands beside the estuary, but beware a rising tide which will force you up over the awkward rocky foreshore.

The main routing goes seaward of the dunes (badly eroded and in the process of reclamation) and follows a stream up left to a post, thereafter veering right and following telegraph poles. Keep round by the fence, cross a footbridge and continue ahead through more dunes and up across the flanks of Brae Hill. At a path fork, drop right then proceed either along the sands or through the back of the dunes.

A recommended alternative from Daymer Bay is via St. Enodoc's church. To reach it, walk left across the well known golf course and follow the marked path. St. Enodoc's dates from the 15th century, with a 13th century spire and has survived inundation by sand which at one time almost completely buried

119

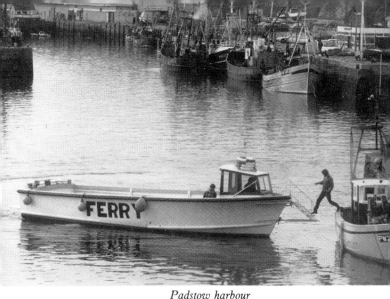

Padstow harbour

it. Excavated and fully restored with assistance from 'The Independent Society for Buildings and Churches', it is associated with the poet John Betjamin, who held this area in great affection and now lies buried in the churchyard. A signed track rejoins the main coast path beyond Brae Hill.

All alternatives eventually converge on the foreshore by Rock's busy sailing school. A ferry to Padstow existed as far back as the 14th century. It is the first of a number of river crossings for the long-distance South West Way walker travelling anti-clockwise. Without ferries (not every river has one!), quite lengthy detours upstream to the first bridge would be involved.

Padstow's harbour is clearly seen across the Camel, but the ferry boat's exact line depends on the state of the tide. Often it will arrive on the sands rather than at a jetty and during exceptionally low spring tides will move down river, not operating from Rock or Padstow themselves. The service is daily every 20 minutes in the season, from 8.00am. to 5.00pm. or later; reduced hours and no Sunday service from October to March. Normally only return fares are issued, but genuine walkers can ask for a single if required.

After an interesting 10 min. ride you will disembark at **PADSTOW** *(all shops, services, and accommodation, including campsite; Tourist Office; car parks; buses to Bodmin Parkway for BR train connections, also* *local services; boat trips; early closing Wednesday).*

Earlier this century, Baddeley and Ward's guidebook to the region stated that '...no one deliberately visits Padstow for its own sake...' Before modern tourism was fully established, working ports like Padstow might have seemed unwelcoming, with few concessions being made for the casual visitor. Indeed, for over a thousand years fishing was its *raison d'être* and even today there is a small fleet, as well as pleasure craft.

The waterfront is a fascinating hub of activity, surrounded by shops and eating establishments - the kind of place that even long-distance walkers will wish to linger in. Apart from its shopping streets and numerous pubs, Padstow's historic buildings are also worth seeking out. The Court House on South Quay once saw Sir Walter Raleigh presiding as Warden of Cornwall. St. Petroc's church at the top of the town is dedicated to a Welsh missionary who landed here in the 6th century, and contains in its churchyard some interesting early Cornish crosses. Prideaux Place, an Elizabethan manor house built in 1598, still belongs to the Prideaux family.

If you happen to visit Padstow on May Day, you will witness its famous Hobby Horse Festival of ancient pagan origin. At most other times the town's pleasant ambience provides coastal walkers with a distinctive change of scene from the largely unfrequented coast path itself. Summer bus services run to nearby coastal villages such as Trevone, Constantine Bay and Porthcothan, enabling good day walks to be undertaken to or from Padstow without the need to retrace steps. In fact, the walking is notably less strenuous now, most of the way to Newquay and beyond for some distance.

SECTION 13 - Padstow to Porthcothan (or Treyarnon)
12 miles (19km)

The River Camel's picturesque southern estuary shores take you out to Stepper Point, whereafter a gradual descent past rock stacks and a collapsed sea cave leads to Trevone. After mostly level walking above low cliffs, an unavoidable beach crossing and a gentle climb, Trevose Head is reached, with its lighthouse conspicuous for many miles along the coast. More flat path ensues past popular sandy beaches between rocky promontories along to Treyarnon and, a little farther on, Porthcothan. Grading – moderate.

Refreshments, shops, some accommodation, toilets and seasonal buses to Padstow at Trevone. Refreshments and toilets at Harlyn Bay. Seasonal refreshments, accommodation, youth hostel and toilets at Treyarnon Beach.

From Padstow's North Quay the onward coast path is signed up a tarred path by a wall, continuing along by a field past the Jubilee Gates and the big stone cross War Memorial. After a tiny luxuriant inlet there are old wartime fortifications on Gun Point, with Doom Bar now clearly in view across the river mouth. The path bends left (west) above dunes and along field edges inland round the back of Harbour Cove. (At low tide it is possible to cut across the sands.) There are adequate waymarks and the path should be cleared of undergrowth, with planks over the boggier bits.

Once past the disused Lifeboat Station, you fork left round Hawker's Cove with its terrace of Coastguard cottages and houses

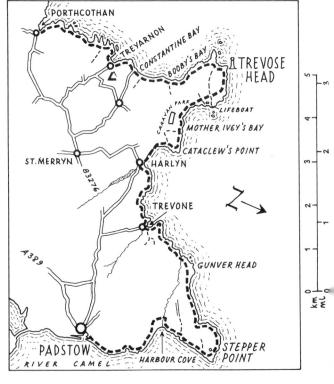

SECTION 13
PADSTOW to PORTHCOTHAN

122

where Padstow's river pilots lived during its heyday as a port. After 50m on a lane, fork right, whereafter more tarmac leads on past buildings to the cliff path. Climbing gently through gorse, the way (which is well walked) reaches a flatter area and takes the middle of 3 paths ahead, rising more steeply to a corner and the Coastguard lookout on **STEPPER POINT** (242ft. - 74m).

By walking on the lower path to a post you get the best sea views, either continuing ahead on the clifftop or climbing back to the 12m-high day mark tower, now unsafe and fenced off. This conspicuous structure was built specifically as a navigation aid for vessels negotiating the Camel estuary and Doom Bar en route for Padstow.

Past some more concrete wartime foundations, Trevose Head attracts attention ahead - a distinctive profile and white lighthouse. From Stepper Point day mark, keep to the seaward path which soon swings left back towards Padstow, past Pepper and Butter holes.

The Camel estuary from dunes near
Harbour Cove

Daymark tower on Stepper Point

Staying on round gorsey clifftops, the route is straightforward and from Gunver Head the next sweep of bay unfolds, as well as rock stacks and islets below, all frequented by seabirds. You drop over a stream, in and out by an overgrown wall and as you cross a field it is worth glancing back to the odd-shaped rocks of Tregudda Gorge and Gunver Head.

Keeping down the cliff edge past the promontory arch of Porthmissen Bridge, you walk past the spectacular 'Round Hole', a collapsed cave into whose recesses the sea surges far below. There has been a steep path to the bottom, but at the time of writing a descent seems too dangerous to recommend.

The coast path angles down to **TREVONE** *(nearby accommodation; cafe; shop; car park; toilets; summer buses to Padstow)* and follows waymarks along by houses and a hotel above extensive rock reefs exposed at low tide. Minor path diversions bypass cliff falls as the sea-front path leads easily on to the popular surfing beach at **HARLYN BAY** *(refreshments; pub; beach shop; car park; toilets)*.

Harlyn was the site of important archaeological discoveries at the turn of the last century. The remains from over 200 burials, including 100 slate coffins in an Iron Age cemetery, were unearthed during house building. Although some items were removed to the British Museum, many were exhibited until recently in a little local museum. That, however, closed and its contents are now in Truro Museum, among them bronze, iron and Celtic gold ornaments.

Cross the road bridge and watch for a sign right to the beach. Unfortunately there is no alternative but to take to the sands for some 350m, so if the tide is very high a delay should be anticipated. Turn up left from the sands to a car park (or cut across Harlyn Bay and scramble up the easy-angled rocks by some red signs at the far side). Keep seaward of a house ('The Cellars'), past a black anchor and on along field edges round Cataclews Point whose quarried blue-grey stone appears widely in the churches of the south-west. Stay seaward towards Mother Ivey's Bay (or Polventon) caravan site - not the most picturesque stretch of path, it must be said - cross a track and continue up by a line of posts. Crossing a stream by the caravan site, walk along its perimeter wall, across a sunken track and over the stile opposite left.

Beyond the next stile and to the left of a house, the path is hemmed in narrowly between chain-link fencing and if you are rucksack-laden you will not wish to meet anyone coming the other way! At the end, go half-right by a garage, over a wall stile and left along by the wall. During the author's last visit, the path was perilously close to the cliff edge in a few places.

Climbing gently . between wall and fence, the way crosses the Lifeboat Station access road and proceeds on uphill along a field edge instead of round the shoreline as one would expect. Prior to 1967, the lifeboat was stationed at Hawker's Cove near Padstow for the 140 years of its busy existence. Another private road is crossed and a stile points the way forward to two posts, the latter on the skyline of **TREVOSE HEAD.**

Walking up, there are exceptional panoramas in clear weather of the coast in both directions - back above the left-hand rock island to the north are the distant radar dishes of Composite Signals Organisation Station near Bude, and Hartland Point some 40 miles (64m) away. To the south, St. Ives is just visible to the naked eye.

The coast path threads between the Coastguard enclosure and the lighthouse (dating from 1847, it is 70ft. - 21m high and waymarked down to the right by posts). There is a short detour out to Dinas Head for those with time to spare. Like Pentire Point and the headlands

125

towards Newquay, Trevose Head is composed of hard igneous rocks. Alternating with them are numerous sandy beaches, not all of which are safe for bathing however, owing to rocks and strong currents.

Walk across the car park, over a stile at its bottom corner, along a stony track then left over a stile and down past another huge 'Round Hole'. The original path was opposite but has become dangerous. An easy descent over heavily grazed pasture leads towards the buildings and vast, grey rock reefs of Booby's Bay. Flat paths soon converge onto the main seafront track past a golf course and many signs warning against the use of inflatables. Several lifeguard huts contain emergency telephones.

The best route forward at **CONSTANTINE BAY** is right across its sands, but high tides will force you to the foot of big dunes. On along the track above low cliffs (car park off left, also buses for Padstow), you traverse grassy Treyarnon Point and arrive at **TREYARNON BEACH** *(accommodation; youth hostel; caravan park; seasonal cafe - Whitsun to September; car park; (toilets).* This is an altogether safer beach with good surfing.

Cross the back of the beach and climb up by houses onto the cliffs. Trethias Island, just offshore, is a Nature Reserve. Keep well back from the eroding cliff edge by a bungalow - its days must be numbered - and proceed on level clifftops past a caravan site. This section closely follows a field wall and if you are pressed for time most of the little headlands can be short-cut. Below them however, are sheer drops to the sea fringed with a succession of caves and arches.

Approaching Porthcothan, the coast path is a ribbon of turf over a planted field - an encouraging sign of a farmer's respect for the walking fraternity; there is also a path nearer the sea. Coming down past a Cornwall Coast Fund collecting box, turn right over the road to arrive at **PORTHCOTHAN** *(accommodation, supplies; seasonal refreshments; telephone; car park; infrequent bus service to Newquay).*

SECTION 14 - Porthcothan to Newquay;   11 miles (18km)

No significant gradients on this stretch, starting with a spectacular passage above the well known rock islands of Bedruthan Steps and continuing along gently undulating cliffs to Mawgan Porth. A short drop to Watergate Beach then an easy 3 mile (5km) walk above the vast sands of Watergate Bay to the urban outskirts of Newquay.   Grading - moderate.

Seasonal refreshments and toilets at the National Trust's Bedruthan Steps Information Centre; also nearby accommodation and campsite. Refreshments, supplies, accommodation, campsite and toilets at Mawgan Porth/Trenance.

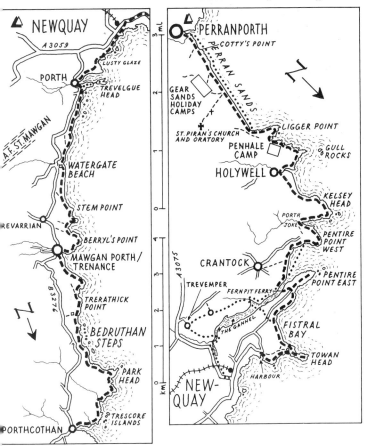

SECTIONS 14 and 15
PORTHCOTHAN to PERRANPORTH

The south side of Porthcothan's sandy inlet has some fine caves worthy of exploration, but the coast path turns in past the Post Office/ Stores and rises gradually past houses. Trescore Islands - a cluster of interesting rock forms just offshore - and pebbly Porth Mear beach precede Park Head, donated to the National Trust by Ernest Thornton-Smith in 1966 for 'Operation Neptune'.

127

Bedruthan Steps from Park Head

Unless dogged by sea mist, you will soon witness a classic piece of Cornish coastal scenery - **BEDRUTHAN STEPS.** Legend has it that the giant Bedruthan used this sequence of large rock islands as stepping stones. Diggory's Island is the first 'step', followed by Queen Bess Rock, said to resemble the monarch's profile before a rock-fall in the early 1980's. Next comes Samaritan Rock, after an East India Company ship of that name wrecked here in 1846, then Redcove Island, Pendarves Island and the conical Carnewas Island.

It seems that a second usage of 'Bedruthan Steps' applies to a long and steep flight of steps down the cliffs between Redcove and Pendarves Island, re-opened in 1975 by the Nationl Trust after closure due to a fatality; erosion remains a threat. *(The National Trust now has an Information Centre/shop/cafe and car parks (toilets) just off the B3276 coast road, open from Easter to end of September. Nearby are a campsite and a few hotels/guesthouses.)*

Undulating now on somewhat less pristine cliffs, the way passes Trerathick Point and High Cove. 2 miles (3.2km) inland stands the tower of St. Eval church, rebuilt as a navigational day mark in the early 1700's and adjacent to a wartime airfield of Coastal Command. R.A.F. St. Mawgan air base is not far away, so the occasional low flying jet can be expected to interrupt the peace! The station's roles include training and the important task of maritime rescue.

Bungalow estates rise from the popular sandy bay and surf beach at **MAWGAN PORTH** *(and* **TRENANCE** *nearby - accommodation; campsite; shop; cafe; pub; Post Office; telephone; car park; toilets; buses for Newquay)*. Tide permitting, it is simplest to walk across the sands, otherwise behind the beach and over the bridge. Follow the coast road uphill for about 100m and turn off right on the cliff path up round Berryl's Point, Beacon Cove then down and up to Griffin's Point which possesses another clear example of Iron Age promontory fortifications, though sadly much has been lost to landslip. In fact, owing to work behind Griffin's Point, the path goes out further than most maps show.

Ahead from Stem Point, Watergate Bay stretches in a great unbroken arc of sand and surf to the outskirts of Newquay 3 miles (4.8km) away. Unless sure of the tides, it is not advisable to walk the beach owing to the danger of becoming cut off beneath the high shale cliffs along whose edge the path winds.

There is a short descent past the salubrious Watergate Bay Hotel to **WATERGATE BEACH** *(hotels; cafe; pub; car park; toilets)*, heavily patronised by surfers. The coast path continues in easy fashion along the cliff edge and before long is closely shadowing the coast road past more burial mounds behind Zacry's Island and Trevelgue Head. Trevelgue Head itself (also called Porth Island) is almost detached from the mainland to which it is connected by footbridge. A short detour is recommended here however, to see possibly the finests 'ciiff castle' in the whole of Cornwall; excavations have yielded evidence of occupation from the Iron Age to the Roman era. Unfortunately there is a dangerous bit of path seaward of the northernmost tumulus and Cornwall County Council advise keeping inland of this.

By now, walkers accustomed to the relative tranquility of life on the trail will be preparing themselves for the urban delights about to be sampled: whether in excited anticipation or dread will depend on individual outlook! During the summer season, Newquay is unashamedly dedicated to tourism - a kind of Cornish Blackpool - and whilst this provides an abundance of amenities and entertainments, the genuine hiker might well feel like a fish out of water! Either side of the short season, Newquay can seem like a ghost town.

Resuming the walk, you can cross Porth sands or walk round the road (there is no coast path as such), proceeding past the Glendorgal Hotel to emerge above Lusty Glaze beach and on along the seafront into the centre of **NEWQUAY** *(all shops, services and accommodation; youth hostel; hospital; bus and coach station; BR station for main line connections at Par; airport; Inshore Rescue Boat; surf board hire, etc; early closing Wednesday).*

The one-time fishing village of Towanblistra acquired its 'new quay' in the 1500's and for the next 300 years increased its trading activity, first in fish and later in more diverse cargoes, including coal imported for use in the Cornish copper and tin mines. Up to the 1920's, local china clay was exported and the railway extended along the line of the main street to the harbour.

With the advent of seaside holidaymaking around the turn of this century, Newquay's prosperity came to rely increasingly upon revenue from visitors who were attracted by its fine sandy beaches and bracing air. Newquay's status as a family resort is well established, but this is also 'Surf Capital' of the UK. The past 3 decades have seen a burgeoning interest in this most exhilarating sport and a sizeable industry now supplies participants (and posers!) with boards, wet suits, clothes and accoutrements. Malibu boards can be hired at Newquay, though there is not always surf to go with them! Swells, wind, tide and the conformation of particular beaches all determine the size and quality of surfing waves.

Although it is possible to walk along the old harbour at low tide, most will tramp the mile or so of busy shopping street through Newquay. By staying close to the coastline beyond the north side of the quay, the path passes the white Huer's Hut from which lookouts would once shout the arrival of pilchard shoals to waiting fishermen. Perhaps only purists will walk from the War Memorial out round Towan Head; otherwise short-cut south along the Headlands Hotel fence from the former Lifeboat Station (1860 -1934).

Fistral Beach, west facing, unusually straight and famed for its surf, can be traversed direct at most tides; the official path skirts a golf course behind it and emerges on a road of hotels and guesthouses at its southern end. Turn right then follow the path around Pentire Point East, or cut down Riverside Crescent and a flight of steps to the Fern Pit ferry.

CHAPTER 3
Newquay to Penzance
(77 miles - 124km)

Crossing the River Gannel, low cliffs connect Crantock Sands with Holywell Bay, backed by enormous dunes. The path is guided through Penhale Army Camp then descends for a splendid, firm beach walk to Perranporth. For many miles ahead, the ruins of old tin and copper mines dot the landscape, both inland and alongside the path, as mineral-bearing granite replaces sandy bays.

St. Agnes Head is rich in wildlife; open heathland leads on past headlands and rocky coves to the holiday settlement of Porth Towan. Outside an M.O.D. area, the walking is tougher along to Portreath; however after one or two steep combes it then becomes mostly easy, passing Hell's Mouth chasm, Godrevy Point's island lighthouse and the Red River at Gwithian before taking to the vast dunes and beach to Hayle Towans. Busy roads at Hayle give way to shady lanes and dunes on the Hayle estuary, bringing you via Carbis Bay to the busy resort of St. Ives.

A long, rugged and remote section of path lies ahead, with accommodation and refreshment places few and far between. It is beautiful, unspoiled coastline and you are walking through an ancient landscape full of archaeological interest. There is rock climbing at Bosigran, but yet more boggy and rocky terrain separates you from Pendeen Watch lighthouse and road access to villages inland.

Further fascinating mine ruins characterise the onward path to Cape Cornwall. The surfing beach of Whitesand Bay leads to Sennen Cove and the redeveloped Land's End complex, whereafter the finest cliff scenery on the entire South West Way can be relished.

Several small coves and beaches beyond Gwennap Head lies Porthcurno with its famous open-air theatre. Increasingly luxuriant vegetation and disused flower fields belie the ground's rocky nature as you descend to St. Loy's bouldery beach and climb over to Lamorna Cove. From the next headland are exciting new views of Mount's Bay. The path reaches Mousehole's popular harbour and follows the coast road to Newlyn and a long seafront promenade to the centre of Penzance.

SECTION 15 - Newquay to Perranporth;   10 miles (16km)

With the River Gannel crossing behind you, Crantock Sands and clifftops lead round to Holywell Bay with its extensive sand dunes and large beach. An army training camp is passed and descent made to Penhale Sands which give good, firm walking for 2½ miles (4km) to Perranporth.   Grading -moderate.

Refreshments, accommodation, supplies and toilets at Crantock, just off route. Refreshments, supplies and toilets at Holywell.

NOTES ON CROSSING THE RIVER GANNEL: Much narrower (only 10m at one point) than the Camel at Padstow, and even wadeable in certain conditions, the River Gannel nevertheless poses a problem for walkers wishing to get beyond Newquay. Wading is only feasible in calm seas when both tide and river are very low - the actual crossing point is directly below the 'e' of Pentire on O.S. Landranger sheet no.200. Nearby is the easiest route over to Crantock Beach - the Fern Pit ferry, which operates from Whitsun to mid-September every day 10.00am. to 6.00pm. During the season, a small slatted footbridge is sometimes installed for low water crossings and an adjacent cafe (seasonal) makes waiting pleasant enough.

About 1km upstream is the second alternative - a ferry to Penpol Creek from below the Penmere Hotel at the bottom of Trethellan Hill. It runs from early June to mid-September during middle and high water. At low tide, a recently extended footbridge over the deeper channel becomes uncovered and Cornwall County Council consider this the official coast path route.

Your third choice requires a different routing through Newquay. Before the railway station and main street (walking west), turn left down Tolcarne Road, past a police station and school. Where the road bends left, keep straight on through a small industrial estate. A path leads out to Edgcumbe Road, along which turn right beneath the railway viaduct and along through roadside gardens. There is a small museum in Trenance Cottages on the right. Cross a road and continue past Trenance boating lake *(cafe)*, at the end of which go right, along Gannel Road (tidal) and in 200m turn left over the footbridge, just where river becomes estuary. From here, follow route directions below.

The only permanently open, all weather and tides crossing of the Gannel is by the main A3075 road to Goonhavern. Once over the river bridge (best reached by bus), turn right on a lane to Trevemper and a footpath via Treringey to Penpol Creek where the main route is picked up.

Newquay's River Gannel at Penpol Creek

Advance warning of tide times can be obtained from a tide table, widely available from newsagents in the area, and from the South West Way Association's annual handbook.

In order to cover the ground for those crossing upstream, walking notes now resume at the footbridge off Gannel Road (option 3 above). Over the river, a broad track runs seaward across grassy mud flats. Faced with a fast rising tide, walkers can either divert sharp left up the track to Trevemper then right on the path via Treringey to Penpol Creek, or follow a path through fields just above the river (not a definitive right of way).

Penpol Creek is easily crossed (aim for rocky steps and a post) except at high water when a short inland detour round its head will lead back to the hedged riverside path along pasture. Opposite are properties of the wealthy, idyllically situated, while pleasure craft will often be seen moored below. It was not always so! The Gannel was busy with trading schooners and the Clemens shipyard in years past and unrealised proposals have been mooted at one time or another for a dammed pleasure lake and for a canal to service the china clay pits.

Rounding a corner, there is a marvellous view ahead across Crantock Sands to the river mouth and lines of surf. If the tide is favourable, branch right before the path starts climbing towards a house:

133

this will take you down a sandy groove to the beach, over a dune and along the sands. Aim to the right of buildings on the skyline and mount easy rocks to a clifftop post. At high tide, follow the path round past a National Trust car park *(cafe/beach shop)*. A reclamation scheme may divert the coast path in future, but at the time of writing you cross an area of sand dunes on the south side of the beach, reaching the stiled cliff path.

There are excellent retrospective views over Pentire Point East to distant Trevose Head with its spine of treacherous rock islands as the coast path proceeds round Pentire Point West over delightful springy turf. Veering inland to pass Porth Joke (locally Polly Joke) by a small footbridge, the conspicuous and much used path left from the back of the beach leads to **CRANTOCK** village *(accommodation; shops, pubs; cafe; campsites; car park; toilets)*, almost a holiday suburb of Newquay.

National Trust signs announce Kelsey Head and Hollywell Bay - our way climbs round grassy clifftops and over a small marshy side valley before Kelsey Head's Iron Age promontory fort is before you. Suddenly the coast is revealed right down to St. Ives and beyond in a sensational foretaste of what is to come. The offshore island in Holywell Bay is Gull (or Carter's) Rocks and a 70 year old wreck is uncovered on the sands at low tide. A gate precedes a boardwalk through gigantic dunes, across which marram grass is being established to stabilise the shifting sandhills threatening the village of **HOLYWELL** *(shops; seasonal cafe; old pub; car park; toilets)*. You can either cross the road bridge and follow Penhale Camp's fence back seaward, or cross the little Treguth River on stepping stones and head

Stranded jellyfish, Crantock Sands

The walk along Penhale Sands

for a large red sign by steps.

An inland diversion through Ellenglaze once bypassed Penhale
Army Training Camp, but a concessionary path now stays close to the
sea. However, it could hardly be described as unrestricted walking!
Signs warn the public to keep seaward of white posts, to heed red flags
and sentries' warnings, not to start grass fires, trespass or take short
cuts. That there are no refreshments or toilets until Perranporth, 5
miles (8km) away, and that care is needed near the cliff edge is true
enough but to call the way 'long and arduous in places' is over the top
for experienced walkers. Arguably such warnings deter non-walkers
from getting into difficulties; in fact, the stretch is an easy one requir-
ing only a modicum of common sense.

The path climbs, keeps left at a fenced mineshaft (high grade iron-
ore was mined during the late 1800's) and weaves seaward of various
installations. Near the camp buildings at Hoblyn's Cove chasm you
are channelled between fences, but Ligger Point restores freedom and
the gradual descent to **PENHALE SANDS** is exhilarating. At first the
path contours very steep grassy cliffside exposed to strong winds.
Keep up left, still following white posts and finally dropping to a
rough track. Turn down right and if the tide is not full an enjoyable

2½ miles (4km) beach walk ensues: Perran Bay sands are the most extensive in the whole of Cornwall and renowned for sand-yachting. At high water, a more tiring switchback through the high dunes or along soft sand may be necessary; there are several escape routes off the sands.

Just before Gear Sands holiday camps, largely unseen, a path leads up to **ST.PIRAN'S ORATORY** and cross - an 8th century chapel now uncompromisingly protected in concrete from encroaching sand but one of Britain's oldest Christian buildings. St. Piran was an Irish missionary and a 12th century church named after him stands not far away to the north-east.

Don't pass the flight of steps to a clifftop path about two-thirds of the way along the beach if the tide is rising as it is possible to get cut off at Cotty's Point. There are however, some impressive caves and old mine workings in sheer, contorted cliffs here.

PERRANPORTH sea front is dominated by the unlovely Ponsmere Hotel and Beach Bar. Cross the river footbridge to its right and walk along to the town *(all shops, services and accommodation; campsite; youth hostel; cafes, restaurants and pubs; buses; car parks; toilets; early closing Wednesday)*.

SECTION 16 - Perranporth to Portreath;   10 miles (16km)

Sandy bays are replaced by granite cliffs and an early encounter with old mine and quarry workings on Cligga Head. After several ups and downs, mine chimneys and ruined engine houses dot the landscape as you approach St.Agnes. St.Agnes Head is renowned for its wildlife, despite a history of industrial exploitation, signs of which are everywhere to see from now on. Leaving Chapel Porth, beach at low tide or cliffs can be walked to Porth Towan, whereafter M.O.D. property keeps the path hugging the cliff edge for a more strenuous 2 miles (3km) before a descent to the harbour and town of Portreath.   Grading - moderate but more difficult in places. Refreshments, accommodation, supplies, telephone and toilets at Trevaunance Cove. Seasonal refreshments and toilets at Chapel Porth. Most shops, services and accommodation at Porth Towan.

After a succession of sandy bays, the coast now changes character abruptly and ahead lie 12 miles (19km) of granite cliffs whose mineral seams were exploited, albeit briefly, a century ago. Thus fine coastal walking is further enhanced by interesting mining relics along the way.

Leave Perranporth on the road south of the beach, past the Cresta Hotel and a small car park, turning left up by the Droskyn Castle

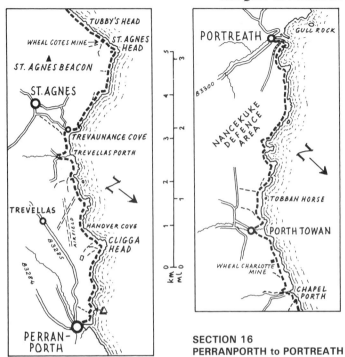

SECTION 16
PERRANPORTH to PORTREATH

Hotel and right into a cul-de-sac lane. Just before the youth hostel sign (a wonderful setting, not unlike Tintagel's), fork up left. At a post, the coast path drops and continues clearly along sheer 250ft (76km) cliffs towards Cligga Head. There are echoes of the Yorkshire Dales in the gravelly path through heather, the traces of mine buildings and piles of spoil.

Recent reclamation work has tended to confuse the onward route at Cligga Head. Passing between two rocky outcrops there are sudden spectacular views, but you have to swing back up left to the clifftop. Official advice is turn left at the ruined building. If lost, any of several easy trods over heather will lead to the correct path ahead.

Little wonder the headland is worse for wear - in addition to mining activity, a large dynamite works (essential to the mining and quarrying industries) was sited here. Last owned by the Nobel company,

137

originator of the Peace Prize, it closed around 1920. The precipitous cove below is named after the brig 'Hanover', wrecked in December 1763 with 27 lives lost, not to mention £60,000 in gold coin which was strenuously salvaged.

Looking back from the path, rock strata contain extraordinary colours, from warm greys and browns to brilliant red-ochres and greens. At the 2nd tarmac track by an old gun position, turn left to a coast path sign, then right. (Inland is Trevellas airfield used now by light aircraft.) Coming round the cliffs there is a dramatic prospect of mine buildings and chimneys dotting the landscape around St.Agnes.

Dropping steeply, the way angles back inland towards the restored engine house chimney at Trevellas Porth. Many eroded paths criss-cross the little combe but moves are afoot by the District Council to remedy the situation and preserve this scene of historical interest for future generations. Tin mining ended here only 60 years ago. Cross the river by the road bridge then turn right off the first bend up a fairly steep stony track to the clifftop.

At a clear path junction by a post, fork down right to Trevaunance Cove *(straight on leads off-route to* **ST.AGNES** *- a worthwhile 1km detour if time permits. Its steep streets, mine buildings and industrial housing vividly evoke a past era and are complemented by 4 good pubs, also accommodation, shops and services; early closing Wed.)*

TREVAUNANCE COVE *(accommodation; restaurant; cafe; pub; shop; telephone; small car park; toilets)*, once a hive of activity from ore shipments and fishing, was never well endowed as a harbour and its quaysides have been all but destroyed by storms over the years. Today, like St.Agnes, it is given over to tourism in a modest way.

Turn right at a coast path sign and almost immediately fork right on a footpath past toilets and along a short stretch of lane servicing houses and hotels. This becomes a level track and beyond garages regains open cliff. You climb steps and zig-zag past posts to the clifftop where a broad stony track is followed, keeping seaward at old spoil heaps, past a bench and on along a pleasant path through heather and gorse.

In earlier years, disused mineshafts were capped with planks covered by soil, but timber is prone to decay with predictably unsatisfactory consequences. Considerable efforts have been made to re-cap them using conical wire shields.

Keep seaward of the coastguard lookout on **ST.AGNES HEAD**, perhaps glancing back for a distant view of an ever receding Trevose Head. Seabirds nesting on the cliffs, Grey seals below and a variety of pathside flora all distinguish St.Agnes Head as an outstanding area for wildlife and remind us that while the ecologically disastrous processes

Wheal Cotes mine ruins

of mining and quarrying decimate creatures and habitats, nature is a great healer. A century ago the area would have been noisy from machinery, scarred with adits and waste, dirty from smoke and discharges which discoloured the adjacent foreshore and sea.

Soon the path reaches the impressive ruins of Wheal Cotes Mine, restored by the National Trust on open heathland of ling, tormentil and bell heather. (St.Agnes Beacon lies not far away to the east and is a premier viewpoint, not only over the immediate landscape but further afield to the south coast around Falmouth and even to St.Michael's Mount near Penzance.) Staying close to the sea, you drop round to **CHAPEL PORTH** *(seasonal beach cafe; car park and toilets on site of tin stamping mill; emergency telephone; Nature Trail)*, an inlet with caves, good sands but dangerous bathing and owned by the National Trust. Those with time to spare could walk back along the beach at low tide to the Towan Roath cliffside shaft and engine house. Also at low tide and with the necessary vigilance, you can walk ahead to Porth Towan just over a mile away.

From the back of the car park a waymarked path continues inland before doubling back. (A very narrow alternative circumvents the southern headland itself - care needed.) At clifftop level again, stay on the right, seaward, path past spoil heaps, eventually passing **Wheal Charlotte** mine and angling down towards a car park at **PORTH TOWAN** *(most shops, services and accommodation; cafes; restaurants; pubs; Post Office; telephones; car parks; toilets.)*

Turn right into West Beach Road then left by Beach View Flats to a coast path sign and a lane rising above the sandy surf beach. This becomes a track onto high, subsiding clifftops, keeping well clear of the crumbling edge above Tobban Horse rock.

At a large obelisk and gate, you join the Nancekuke Defence Area perimeter fence (a smaller version of the original!), whose unwelcome company persists for 2 miles (3km). The walking becomes wilder and more strenuous, locked between fence and precipitous cliffs as you drop through a steep combe by a small lake and waterfall. Gull Rock, off Portreath, hoves into sight ahead and after another deep stream valley the fence swings away left at a gate and white pole. Round the cove beyond Gooden Heane Point, the cliff edge is extremely unstable but there follows a plain choice between a path round the conspicuous daymark or the road direct down to **PORTREATH** *(all shops, services and accommodation; buses; car parks; toilets; Crazy Golf etc! early closing Wed.)*

New housing here seems rather out of character, though in truth Portreath owes more to the habits and needs of modern visitors than to its traditional harbour trades serving the Camborne and Redruth mines. Its heyday spanned the last half of the 18th century, but the harbour's much needed inner basin, built in the mid-1800's, did greatly facilitate exports of copper and imports of coal subsequently. Fishing, too, continues despite this coast's exposure to fierce weather and heavy swells which have always reduced Portreath's effectiveness as a safe port for shipping.

SECTION 17 - Portreath to Hayle; 12 miles (19km)

After climbing to the clifftops and negotiating a steep combe, there is level walking high above the sea along Reskajeage Downs, never far from the coast road. Passing the sensational Hell's Mouth chasm, you follow fields out round Navax and Godrevy Points for superb views of the coast and Godrevy lighthouse on its rock island. The aptly named Red River is crossed at Gwithian village where a seaward turn takes you through the vast dune system of Upton Towans and along the sands to Hayle Towans at the far end. Skirting old industrial buildings, the path joins the main A30 road at Hayle. Grading - moderate.

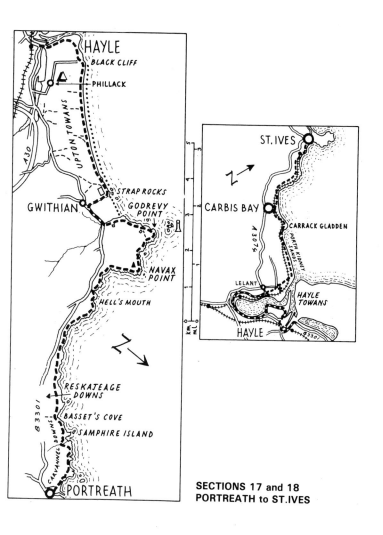

SECTIONS 17 and 18
PORTREATH to ST.IVES

141

Godrevy lighthouse

Seasonal cafe at Hell's Mouth. Seasonal cafe and toilets near Godrevy Point. Pub (meals) by Red River. Accommodation, campsites, pub and telephone at Gwithian. Refreshments and supplies at Upton Towans. Pub and cafe at Hayle Towans.

Across Portreath's bridge, turn right up a sloping lane past houses and over to a bungalow/chalet development where the coast path is signed left up a small valley. At the top, either walk round the headland (possible sightings of Grey seals) or turn left along Carvannel Downs. Waymarks delineate a sensible improved route down and up steep Porth-Cadjack Cove adjacent to Samphire Island. (Samphire is an edible cliff plant with aromatic, saline, fleshy leaves once gathered for pickling.)

The next combe behind Basset's Cove is altogether gentler, leading via a car parking area onto the plateau-like Reskajeage Downs. There are airy views down the sheer edge of land to a rugged foreshore, but otherwise the walking is less interesting than of late - less energetic too! Eyes may well rest on higher ground inland: rising above the Redruth/Camborne conurbation is the Carn Brea ridge, topped by a conspicuous monument to Lord Dunstanville erected in 1836. Farther ahead lie the windswept granite hills of West Penwith pointing towards Land's End.

Good level walking continues along field edges, converging

eventually with the B3301 coast road before swinging right, through gorse and round the seaward boundary of Hudder Down. There is a cafe (seasonal) and car park on the road at **HELL'S MOUTH** - an awesome 200ft (61m) vertical chasm peered into by many a passing holidaymaker in the summer season and a breeding ground for guillemot, razorbill, fulmar and kittiwake.

Now the coast path joins a wider one and you turn right, with Upton Towans dunes and St.Ives visible away to the left. Cross a stile into a field by the right of 2 gates, and the next stile will lead you on through gorse. Navax Point is a haze of bluebells in springtime and is also a fine spot for birdwatching, especially in the summer and autumn when shearwaters, fulmars and gannets may be seen flying west in large numbers.

In sight for so long, Godrevy lighthouse is at last near to hand. (If time presses, a short cut to the headland car park can be made over a stile in a fence corner on the left.) Walking round **GODREVY POINT** affords exciting views of the island lighthouse, constructed in 1859 but now unmanned and automatic. A treacherous reef known as The Stones had previously claimed many vessels, including the well known wreck of 1649 in which the entire possessions of the refugee Prince of Wales were lost en route for France, on the very day of his father's (Charles I) execution; all but 2 of the crew perished.

Walking south from the point you soon reach the large, grassy National Trust car park *(summer cafe; toilets.)* To reach Gwithian Towans at Strap Rocks across the mouth of Red River (aptly named from a suspension of tin-ore from South Crofty Mine near Camborne in its waters), the official path takes to the road past Godrevy Sand Works and the Sandsifter pub *(meals.)* If tide and river are very low, you can cut straight across the beach. Turn right over the B3301 road bridge and up into the sleepy village of **GWITHIAN** *(accommodation; several nearby campsites; pub; telephone,)* with its picturesque thatched cottages and interesting old churchyard containing the graves of local shipwreck victims.

Turn right before the church, by the side of the Glencoe House Hotel on a sandy lane through dunes and by a holiday camp *(General Stores; car park; refreshments)*, then swinging parallel to the sea on an undulating and tortuous grassy path. If the tide allows, walking is easier on the vast, firm beach - keep right on along the 2 miles (3km) sweep of sand until you come to 2 wartime pillboxes just below Black Cliff, one bearing a lifeguard hut. Here you rejoin the high water route.

Upton Towans' extensive dune system, unlike Braunton Burrows of

143

similar size in North Devon, is bisected by numerous tracks and dotted with chalets, bungalows and caravans. In very windy conditions, blowing sand can make walking the beach or dunes area exceptionally unpleasant and at such times the author suggests following the B3301 and the A30 (pavement) to Hayle.

Leaving the beach at Black Cliff, the path is hard to define as it penetrates a settlement of bungalows and chalets at **HAYLE TOWANS** *(pub; beach shop/cafe):* steer a middle route between the beach and higher land behind. When the coast path was inaugurated, a ferry plied from here across the Hayle estuary, but alas no longer does so. You are forced to skirt a disused power station and various dilapidated buildings before crossing the canal basin bridge and meeting the main A30 road at **HAYLE** *(all shops, services and accommodation; youth hostel at Phillack - 750m east of the canal bridge; cafe, restaurants and pubs; buses and trains for St.Ives - main line connections at St.Erth; car park; toilets; early closing Thurs.)*

A working port and hotch-potch of small industry and commerce, Hayle sits astride a busy trunk road. It was described by Black's Guide at the turn of the last century as dirty, squalid and uninteresting, but do not be disheartened by this sudden decline in walking quality. Noise and fumes are soon left behind for quieter surroundings to St.Ives, then an outstandingly remote and unspoilt stage to Land's End - a fitting climax to hiking on the north coast.

SECTION 18 - Hayle to St. Ives;   7 miles (11km)

A short and easy walk, but beyond St. Ives accommodation and supplies are harder to come by. Unpleasant road walking is necessary to clear Hayle, but soon a delightful, flowery lane is taken to Lelant where a golf course gives access to dunes alongside the branch railway from St. Erth to St. Ives. Undulations above sands bordering the Hayle estuary then leafy residential lanes lead down to St. Ives. (With some forward planning if time is short, this section could be extended to Zennor.)   Grading - easy. Refreshments and accommodation at Carbis Bay.

The busy A30 bends left then turns sharply right beneath Hayle's railway viaduct *(station up left)* at a bad junction for pedestrians with the B3302. Continuing past the harbour however, watch for a sign pointing right to the Weir and leading round a rough embankment enclosing Carnsew Pool. This is a more pleasant detour, providing opportunities to view seabirds and waders in the estuary. For rapid onward progress, keep to the road which mercifully has a pavement.

At the White Inn *(restaurant)*, turn right to pass the Cornucopia

The coast path opposite Hayle Towans

entertainments centre and a Garden Centre on the left. Keep right at the mini-roundabout and at the top of the rise ahead turn right by an ancient stone cross under a large tree and sign 'Woodlands'. Virtually traffic-free, this peaceful by-road wanders alongside colourful flowers and shrubs and a Woodland Trust copse. (There can be few railway trips in the country as scenic as that from Lelant Saltings 'park-and-ride' station to St. Ives. The branch opened in 1877 and was the last broad gauge line to be built in England.)

Topping a rise, turn right at the junction (at the author's last visit, here was the first coast path waymark sign since Gwithian) and walk down the path between **LELANT'S** mainly 15th century St. Uny's church and the churchyard. With Godrevy lighthouse now part of the retrospective coastscape, notices warn walkers about the perils of golf and may leave you wishing you'd brought a hard hat! You drop under a small railway bridge and swing left by the Ferry House (where you would have emerged had a ferry been running!), proceeding along dunes just right of the railway track above lovely Porth Kidney Sands (dangerous bathing).

The coast path undulates behind screens of branches heavy with blossom in spring, round to Carrack Gladden, whereafter the seaward path is the better of two alternatives, although if unsure it is unlikely you will get lost. The more inland path crosses the railway and they both converge anyway at the Carbis Bay Hotel *(beach shop/cafe)*. Turn right onto the sea front then climb to cross the railway bridge, continuing along leafy, almost tropical residential lanes. Over the railway once more and you are descending to Porthminster beach. Ahead lies the harbour and up left the town of **ST. IVES** *(all shops, services and accommodation; campsite; bus services; BR station for main line connections at St. Erth; car parks; museum; boat trips; 4 good beaches, etc; early closing Thursday).*

St. Ives' sometimes turbulent history dates back to AD460 when the missionary St. Ia, daughter of an Irish chieftain, landed here and gave her name to the settlement. On 'The Island', north of the town centre, can be found the restored Chapel of St. Nicholas, once a shipping beacon and from which there are good views of the little isthmus. Well protected from prevailing swells and weather by St. Ives Head, the east-facing harbour forms a focal point for visitors; its quaysides and mole were built around 1770 by Smeaton, who also constructed the Eddystone lighthouse.

For the majority of visitors, St. Ives epitomises Cornwall. Often thought of in recent times as an artists' mecca, emphasis has shifted to

Approaching St. Ives

crafts which are well represented here. There can be no doubting that tourism is the town's lifeblood, as it has increasingly become since the railway brought access to this remote southern outpost of Britain. 500 years of pilchard fishing finally came to an end in the 1890's due to climatic changes.

Overrun by holidaymakers during the brief summer season, St. Ives can seem deserted at other times of the year. In this it has much in common with other Cornish resorts which suffer a kind of fossilisation during the winter. Shrinking indigenous populations are being replaced by elderly retired folk who, through no fault of their own, often swamp what youthful energy these places once possessed.

SECTION 19 - St. Ives to Pendeen Watch (Boscaswell); 13 miles (21km)

Though not especially far, a rugged and strenuous walk along remote coastline and awkward underfoot at times. Soon leaving the holiday crowds behind, you engage a series of minor ascents and descents over rocky and often boggy ground. Cove follows headland as the path weaves its way above the sea to Zennor Head. Walking through an ancient landscape, you pass Iron Age earthworks and mining ruins towards distant Pendeen Watch lighthouse. Bosigran Cliff is a rock climbing playground heavily patronised in summer. More awkward and boggy going precedes a welcome flatter stretch before the final combe and beach below Pendeen Watch. Grading -strenuous.

Pub and limited accommodation off route at Zennor. Refreshments off route at Gurnard's Head Hotel. Seasonal refreshments and campsite off route at Bosigran Farm.

NOTE: At no other point on the entire South West Way (except perhaps at Hartland Quay before the walk to Bude) is it more imperative to take stock of your individual situation. Ahead stretch 22 miles (35km) of rugged coast with no on-route accommodation or refreshments other than a seasonal cafe booth at Cape Cornwall car park. Whilst it is possible to detour inland for a bed or a meal around Zennor, Porthmeor, Boscaswell and St. Just, and whilst it is also true that the B3306 coast road is never more than 2 miles (3km) away, most of this long stage is empty and remote. The going is quite rough in places too, so it is a stretch to be reckoned with in every sense.

Certainly food, drink, emergency rations, spare sweater and shell clothing should be carried and a weather forecast consulted before setting out - rain, mist, headwinds and even unmitigated sunshine can all slow your progress down. Accommodation off-route should be

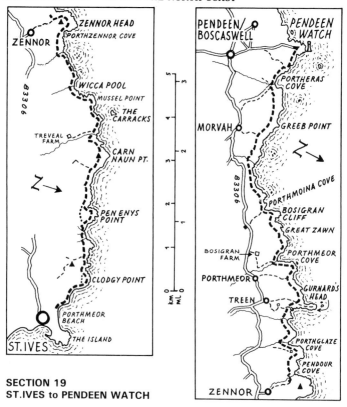

SECTION 19
ST. IVES to PENDEEN WATCH

booked in advance if you are travelling in high season. By the same token, you will meet only genuinely interested walkers along the way and, apart from in adverse weather, it is as grand a coastal hike as you will find anywhere in the UK.

To leave St. Ives, walk over to north-facing Porthmeor Beach. A metalled path leads out past putting and bowling greens above low cliffs, a very popular local stroll, but after a coast path sign to Zennor 6½ miles (10.5km), the way becomes more rugged. Choose the seaward of various trods and when you reach a short coast path waymark, either go right round Clodgy Point or left up behind it.

Reversing the status quo of most coastal topography, headlands on

this stage have to be descended to - sometimes unexpectedly steeply
-and invariably the path grows more awkward towards the foreshore.
Undulating, rocky and sometimes boggy underfoot, this is prime
ankle-twisting country!

At the top of rocky steps stands an incongruous metal squeeze-stile
and a finger post pointing the way ahead. Several streams are crossed
before Pen Enys Point (National Trust) is rounded, another
waymarking post aiding navigation. Paving slabs have been laid over
bog, and in one place a section of duckboarding which, although more
costly to install, at least preserves the flora beneath it. Some fence post
tops are painted dull orange to help route finding - reassuring in mist
-but growing interest in coastal walking has resulted in the path being
quite well used compared to a decade ago.

Terrain eases for a while and at a finger post by a gate there is
possible access left to a country lane at Trevessa Farm (about a mile)
The triangulation pillar on **CARN NAUN POINT** (318ft. - 97m) is
right by the path so an exact measure of progress can be made even in
the worst visibility. However, in clear conditions there are open views
all round for the first time. Inland hills reach over 700ft. (220m) but
appear much higher, their slopes bearing prolific signs of earlier
occupation by man - Iron Age hill forts, standing stones, burial
mounds, stone circles and ancient village sites. Offshore, the Carracks
Reef is reputed to be a haunt of seals while in the distance ahead
stands the castle-like profile of Gurnard's Head. In exceptionally clear
air, sightings are possible back to St. Agnes Beacon and, believe it or
not, to Trevose Head!

River Cove - the next descent - has a fine waterfall and could offer
wild pitching for backpackers; the path up left is to Treveal Farm.
Beyond the climb out and a succession of small rocky inlets, a waymark shows the path dropping round Mussel Point; at times the flora
is more reminiscent of rock gardens than virgin clifftop.

As you turn the corner on Mussel Point, a dramatic bay is revealed,
backed by a bouldery foreshore. During rough weather and high tides
you could get wet from spray as the path meanders along the back of
Wicca Pool. Veering inland to cross a stream, Tremedda Cliffs are
precipitous and riven with indentations, one of which - Porthzennor
Cove - is climbed above seaward to gain **ZENNOR HEAD.**

Given to the National Trust in December 1953 by A.B. 'in memory
of the friends who have sustained me', Zennor Head is doubly significant for the walker who seeks a meal or overnight halt. With Pendeen
Watch still a rugged 6 miles (9.5km) away, the coast path heads
towards **ZENNOR** village *(limited accommodation; pub; telephone;*

Gurnard Head (top right) from Zennor Head

Cornish Life Museum). If you wish to visit it, keep straight on over a large stone stile where the coast path swings right. The church (mainly 15th century) is well worth visiting for its memorials, Cornish crosses and mermaid pew carvings. A mile or so to the south-east is found Zennor Quoit, a Neolithic stone burial chamber.

Surrounding Zennor is an ancient landscape whose massive walls built of uneven granite blocks almost deny the hand of man in their making. Here and there a herd of cows or solitary horses bring movement to the ageless silence.

From the stone stile, turn right down steps by a Coastguard bungalow, round its little vegetable garden, down over a stream engulfed by exotic vegetation and climb left to a finger post on the skyline (not straight ahead). You will pass a bench installed in memory of Denys Val Baker, author, editor and seafarer, above Pendour Cove. On the next minor promontory there is a fine view back to Zennor Head, then you drop to a wall above lichen-covered rocks and climb to another waymark post and rocky outcrop.

Veering inland to round a dramatic cleft and waterfall behind Porthglaze Cove, buildings and ruins below Treen appear ahead. Down over a footbridge, you cross the lower dwelling's access track and pass an impressive ruined mine engine house above Treen Cove. As the path climbs inland of **GURNARD'S HEAD'S** distinctive rocky spine, another good path will be met leading out to the headland itself, with its Iron Age cliff castle and splendid vantage points. Of equal, or perhaps conflicting interest might be a 750m detour inland to the Gurnard's Head Hotel at Treen - one of precious few places of refreshment accessible to the coastal walker hereabouts!

Cresting a rise, Pendeen Watch lighthouse seems a little closer, though terrain and route conspire to slow up westerly progress tantalisingly. At the next inlet - Porthmeor Cove - are pinnacled granite, mountain-like hillsides and a footbridge of hefty slabs. (*During the season there is a diversion left to Bosigran Farm for cream teas, crafts, campsite and a tin mine - about 750m off route.*) The onward path is boggy, churned up by cattle and altogether less clear, but small signs help navigation, aiming up to a stile.

You can peer down to Great Zawn, but soon there is a climb over broken slopes of shattered rock, up inland past a seat, through a wall and out onto the slabby summit of **BOSIGRAN CLIFF**. It is easy to go astray here owing to numerous trods well used by rock climbers and trippers - the coast road is only a few hundred metres away.

The coast path drops left behind Porthmoina Cove where a track leads on up to the B3306 (*mountain rescue kit, regional Climbers' Club hut and Bosigran Farm - see above*). A National Trust sign urges you to report by telephone horseriding, camping etc. which it is keen to discourage. In fairness, the area is already so heavily used by climbers and sightseers that any additional activities would create serious environmental damage.

Unless time is of the essence, this is an entertaining spot to linger in - Bosigran Cliffs are one of the best known rock climbing playgrounds in Cornwall. From the coast path, which climbs parallel to a fence and wall past a curious enclosure, there are grandstand views over granite pinnacles and beetling rock faces festooned with climbers at various stages of ascent.

Knobbly and rugged, our path passes a direction post and a mine ruin of walls and mounds above Greeb Point (*Morvah hamlet lies 750m along a sunken path off left - buses for St. Just and Penzance in the summer*). The accustomed bogginess persists, aided and abetted by cattle and springs. Alongside more ancient field walls there is welcome flat walking for a while over low gorse and heather, Pendeen Watch still a combe away.

Eventually a wider path (from Morvah) is met, turning down right to Portheras Cove, small and shelving but the first sandy beach since St. Ives. A sign warns against walking barefoot on the sands due to razor sharp metal fragments from a wreck blown up in an attempt to improve the environment! The offending particles may not be visible on the surface but numerous holidaymakers who ignored the warnings have ended up in Casualty at Truro Hospital. An emergency telephone is provided!

Zig-zags down to cross the stream are followed by a scramble out and a concrete path angling easily uphill. You drop over grass above slipway sheds then turn left up the access track past a gravel car park and along by the lighthouse walls at **PENDEEN WATCH**.

Immaculately painted in black and white, the lighthouse was opened in 1900 and owes its existence to the particularly lethal stretch of coast upon which it stands. Exposed from south-west round to north-east and fringed with offshore rocks and reefs, it had caused wrecks unacceptably often during the last century when shipping was used extensively to shift ores and coal. Even so, the St. Ives lifeboat was lost in a severe gale in January 1939, only one of its eight crew surviving.

Walk inland up the lane for 400m, turning off it to the right at a stone coast path sign opposite a row of white cottages. This lane leads on to **HIGHER BOSCASWELL/PENDEEN** and the coast road. *(The village contains a General Store; accommodation - including campsite at Trevellard; pub; restaurants; Post Office and telephone, but is a mile off route; early closing Thursday).* There is another access point from the coast path a little further on.)

SECTION 20 - Pendeen Watch to Porthcurno;   15 miles (24km)

Derelict mining installations dominate this section of path at first and a working tin mine lies close by. An inland crossing of a stream valley and return to the coast brings you to Cape Cornwall, the only such feature in England and Wales. Dropping through another combe, you regain clifftop level with fine views before traversing rocky slopes to Whitesand Bay - a popular surfing beach leading along to Sennen Cove. Several well worn tracks cross level clifftops to the newly redeveloped Land's End complex, but walkers pay no entry fee to stay on the coast path which now provides access to an area of exceptional natural beauty. Past much photographed offshore rocks and cliff formations along to Mill Bay and Gwennap Head, some considerable downs and ups are met as you drop to coves and small beaches, finally reaching the famous open air theatre and a very steep descent to Porthcurno.   Grading - moderate but more difficult here and there.

Seasonal refreshments off route at Geevor Mine. Seasonal refreshments and

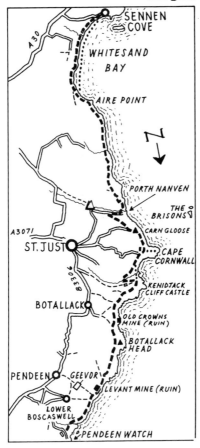

SECTION 20
PENDEEN WATCH to SENNEN COVE

possible B&B in the Kenidjack valley. Seasonal refreshments and toilets at Cape Cornwall. Youth hostel just inland at Letcha Vean. Refreshments, supplies and accommodation at Sennen Cove/Sennen. Refreshments, accommodation and toilets at Land's End. Seasonal refreshments and toilets at Porthgwarra.

153

Derelict installations - Levant Mine

Our onward path from the lane above Pendeen Watch now crosses a marshy valley and continues through the derelict installations of **LEVANT MINE**. Mining activity was intense in this area as ores were discovered close to the surface. Where the igneous granite had once intruded into sedimentary rocks, liquids and gases were formed which ultimately solidified into minerals such as copper and tin. Levant Mine was a major producer of tin and copper ore for over a century until, following a tragedy in which the man-engine failed and 31 miners died, it finally closed in 1919. The main shaft was 2,000ft. (600m) deep and workings extended for a mile beneath the sea bed; one of the steam-driven beam engines has been preserved for posterity by the National Trust.

Mining ruins may dominate the ensuing section of path, but the distant hum of machinery belongs to a working tin mine - **GEEVOR**. During the 1960's, the then flooded Levant Mine was rescued by Geevor and a concrete plug inserted to seal the breach. Geevor is now exploiting the Levant reserves and those of nearby Boscaswell Mine. *(For guided tours of the surface workings, museum and cafe, take the track up left above Levant Zawn to the coast road and turn left for a few hundred metres to Geevor's entrance.)*

Passing 3 chimneys, the stony track reaches a finger post below

154

Mine ruins near Botallack Head

which stands the Levant Beam Engine. The path crosses a metalled lane and continues, wide and stony, past a shorter chimney on the left. Stay on the main track past another small ruin ahead: across from derelict buildings on the right is the trig. pillar on Botallack Head. 200m farther on, go right along by a wall to a waymark post near a chimney stump, turning left by it and returning onto a clear track. There is a finger post on the right and down below are the dramatic, restored engine houses of Old Crowns Mine on a rocky ledge above the sea - a classic view and much photographed. The mine was visited by the Prince and Princess of Wales in 1865 and today the upper ruins are a favourite picnic spot for visitors.

You will pass some large concrete walls which at the author's last visit were daubed with graffiti - an apparently inevitable consequence of public motor access. **BOTALLACK** village is a short distance inland *(pub; car park; telephone; campsite)*. 2 more ruined winding houses and numerous overgrown heaps of stones and old walls lead on to where you join a path from the left at a conspicuous post by an impressive ruin on the right. At the next waymark, bear off right on a

Cape Cornwall

grassy path over gorse. St. Just, a larger settlement, lies to the south-east.

Rounding a corner, you are suddenly confronted by Kenidjack cliff castle in the foreground, Cape Cornwall beyond, and excitingly (if visibility allows) the Longships lighthouse and rocks off Land's End. Keep left of the Iron Age cliff castle ramparts and ditch, dropping to a track going inland. (It is possible to make a direct crossing of the Kenidjack valley by walking 20m to seaward and dropping steeply through mine spoil. Cross the stream at its mouth on boulders and climb out to meet the official path at Porth Ledden.)

The main route follows the track for about 100m to a triple sign (a slight case of overkill?), at which fork down right, over a stile then left along a grassy path. *(In summer, the nearby cottage provides soft drinks, tea and coffee, B&B.)* The coast path veers right over a small bridge amidst luxuriant undergrowth then zig-zags steeply up through drifts of bluebells in springtime, heading back for the coast. Walking along above Porth Ledden you meet a road and turn down right to the car park *(toilets; refreshments in season)* at **CAPE CORNWALL**.

Cape Cornwall's slopes are under cultivation; the prominent, almost futuristic structure on its summit is a chimney for the Cape Cornwall Mine which closed in 1878. This headland (the only cape in England and Wales) is marginally east of Land's End's latitude but was thought to be England's most westerly point in previous centuries. There is a walk out to its tip (yet another Iron Age defensive position) if you have time, otherwise walk across the cape's neck, down steps and up to a rough track. Turn sharp right up past cottages to regain the clifftop. Here we meet a minor road but turn off right by a bench on a path opposite the trig. pillar on Carn Gloose.

The buildings on Land's End itself are now visible beyond Whitesand Bay and Sennen Cove, though still 5 miles (8km) of moderately rough walking away. 1km offshore are the infamous Brisons, scene of many shipwrecks. About 75m further along the road may be found a mid-Bronze Age chambered cairn, thought to have been some kind of religious shrine and one of the most enigmatic of Cornwall's many archaeological sites, despite being visually disappointing.

Continue down the path well inland (dangerous mineshaft below in the bracken). Land's End youth hostel, housed in an erstwhile mine manager's dwelling, lies a short way up the valley, but the coast path turns right on the tarmac lane to the stream mouth at **PORTH NANVEN**, notable for its raised beach. Cross the stream and climb steps to a rocky corner (path left to St. Just), then proceed on up through rocks past more dangerous mineshafts to the clifftop; the path

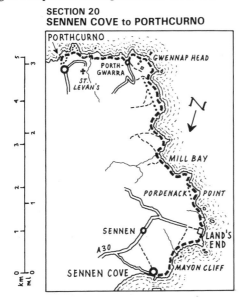

SECTION 20
SENNEN COVE to PORTHCURNO

Sennen Cove - huddled against the Atlantic

here is well made and waymarked. From these high cliffs there are outstanding views in all directions.

Once over the next rise, you angle down over grass to a stile then down further to plank bridges and up steeply to a rocky outcrop. The way now undulates along sloping cliffside then you are scrambling through two spurs of granite blocks in quick succession approaching Aire Point. Soon it is necessary to exercise great caution, for the cliff edge is seriously eroding round this end of Whitesand Bay exposed to south-west storms. At the first sandy beach, a path climbs left to a lane and campsites; bathing is dangerous - emergency telephone. Unless the tide is out, the onward path takes a sandy course above the beach and weaves up through boulders, becoming knobbly and awkward underfoot. It is easiest to walk along the sands, popular with surfers - otherwise go slightly inland through the dunes to arrive at **SENNEN COVE** *(shops and services; accommodation - campsites nearby and at Sennen a mile away; restaurants, cafes and pubs; telephone; buses for Penzance and Land's End; car parks; toilets; early closing Thursday).*

This much visited former fishing harbour faces north but still receives spectacular seas; at such times, when swells crash over jetty and foreshore, one experiences a vivid sense of vulnerability faced with the Atlantic Ocean's awesome forces.

Land's End from the Coast Path

Walk past the Lifeboat Station, below which stands an interesting round capstan house once used to winch boats up the slipway, and continue through the car park. Turn left at the toilets to a coast path sign and on up past the Coastguard lookout onto Mayon Cliff. The easy, well walked track over to Land's End is heralded by a large sign - 'Cliffs and sea are natural hazards and a potential danger. Please be careful' - which may prompt wry smiles from long-distance walkers who, whether in stages or in one marathon trek, have negotiated real danger and difficulties along the 240 miles (386km) from Minehead.

In fact the way soon bifurcates, a right fork leading to the 'First and Last House', straight on to the car park and main entrance. Coastal walkers will stay closest to the sea past the National Trust's Iron Age Maen Castle and Dr. Syntax's Head. The latter is actually the UK's (excluding Ireland) most westerly point, named after a fictional character from a late 19th century book by William Coombes entitled *Dr. Syntax in Search of the Picturesque'*.

LAND'S END (*hotel accommodation - more in the village; meals and drinks; souvenirs; audio-visual displays; exhibitions; 'The Last Labyrinth'; Galleon play area; car park; toilets; buses to Penzance*) has recently undergone a massive £4 million facelift which, as well as extending amenities, has also established a much needed element of architectural homogeneity. In place of the old flag-flying fairground razzmatazz which always seemed in danger of pandering to the lowest common denominator of taste, Land's End now has more to offer as a family day out. As such, the crowds are likely to increase, but coastal walkers will be free from any charge and can choose to eschew it all by taking one of the southbound paths. Within a few minutes it is all a memory and from a walker's standpoint what follows is unsurpassed in natural beauty and drama on the whole South West Way.

Apart from man-made attractions, there is much to look at in terms of coastal and ocean scenery around Dr. Johnson's Head. Offshore rocks with names like Kettle's Bottom and Shark's Fin are best viewed through binoculars, though Longships and even Wolf Rock lighthouses can be seen with the naked eye. In very clear air, The Isles of Scilly may be picked out 28 miles (45km) to the south-west. The present Longships lighthouse, built in 1873 and rising 110ft. (33m) above the sea, supercedes an earlier version which lasted only 80 years.

Gazing westwards, nothing but ocean separates you from America and this uninterrupted fetch endows Atlantic waves with unfettered power; in rough weather the whole area can be veiled with salt spray. Even though sea level is accessible with a little scrambling in calm conditions, it is generally considered unwise to linger there as freak waves are known to occur from time to time and have been responsible for several tragic deaths.

Numerous paths have been worn around Land's End - the official line is somewhat inland but others exist nearer the cliff edge overlooking the castellated Armed Knight and arched Enys Dodman rock islands. As the modern buildings and the press of humanity recede quickly behind you, the walking environment is spectacularly beautiful. Cove follows granite headland, each with a visual treat in store as the coast path meanders along past Pordenack Point above an infinite variety of rock forms, perched boulders and pinnacled ridges. No words or pictures can match the animation of glittering swells and turquoise shallows seen beyond a foreground of yellow gorse and purple heather.

Lichen bearing rocks and a mine shaft precede Mill Bay (or Nanjizal), a bouldery, sandy beach whose stream the coast path crosses at an old mill wheel pit before climbing steeply to the right up steps to the clifftop. The way now undulates straightforwardly above Pendower, Folly and Porth Loe coves to the Coastguard lookout on the great buttressed mass of **GWENNAP HEAD** *(Mountain Rescue Post, mainly for rock climbers on the nearby sea cliffs)*. Gwennap Head's Cornish name is Tol-Pedn-Penwith - the Holed Headland - from the collapsed sea cave at its apex (not marked on maps).

Assuming you are on the upper path, keep ahead to the buildings and road, turning up right then left past a red cone and black and white tower. These day marks warn shipping of the treacherous Runnel Stone Reef a mile out to sea, also marked by a whistling buoy in windy weather. The rock was 'decapitated' on October 8th 1923 when the 6,173 ton 'City of Westminster' struck it, breaking off the top 20ft. or so and rendering it less of a hazard than hitherto!

Down into the dimimutive fishing hamlet of **PORTHGWARRA** *(last refreshments for many miles; car park; toilets)*, you will pass through a rock tunnel, used with the slipway for launching boats in rough weather. Turn right by Cove Cottage, left at an old finger post and right at the next one, now on a rocky path at first between banks then out onto clifftop round Carn Scathe. Fork right then drop through a valley past St. Levan's Holy Well in a tiny walled enclosure. The Norman church of St. Levan stands approximately 400m inland and is worth visiting for its unusual features and details. Although the descent and subsequent climb out from Porthchapel are considerable and its sandy beach dangerous in rough seas, it is nevertheless a delightful and secluded spot.

There now follows an optional detour round the National Trust

Above Porthcurno

headland of Pedn-Mên-An-Mere before arriving above the well known Minack Open Air Theatre *(car park)*. Founded by Miss Rowena Cade in 1935, the auditorium was constructed from a natural amphitheatre high on the cliffs. During the summer, productions are put on weather permitting, but at other times you can view the theatre for a small charge.

A notice diverts children and the elderly onto a safer descent to **PORTHCURNO** *(some accommodation up inland; car park; toilets)*, the coastal route dropping very abruptly on rock steps almost vertically above the sea - somewhat disconcerting in strong winds with a backpack! Porthcurno boasts a cable and wireless engineering school owing to its importance as a terminus for submarine cables; the first such link with India was routed ashore here in 1870.

SECTION 21 - Porthcurno to Penzance;   10 miles (16km)

Climbing to the clifftops, you pass a track to Treen village and a 'logan stone and drop to picturesque Penberth Cove. Soon after, the rocky path makes a big descent into a wild combe with an equally steep exit. Pretty woods surround secluded St. Loy settlement where you take to the bouldery beach before ascending boggy cliffside to Boscawen Point, whereafter the undulating path approaches Tater-du lighthouse. Awkward rocky terrain masked by lush vegetation brings you to Lamorna Cove and out to a splendid granite headland with views across to Mount's Bay. After following low cliffs, there is a tortuous stretch through overgrown cultivation terraces and a climb over to the popular harbour town of Mousehole. The official way onward to Newlyn uses the coast road past a dusty quarry, but fishing quaysides and a delightful promenade leading to Penzance form an interesting and pleasant end to this North Coast route.   Grading - more difficult. Refreshments, accommodation (including campsite) and toilets off route at Treen. Refreshments, accommodation and toilets at Lamorna Cove. Most shops, services and accommodation, buses to Penzance at Mousehole. All shops, services and accommodation at Newlyn.

The coast path leads you left inland round Porthcurno's vegetated back, across the main beach access track, very busy in season, and on ahead at a marker stone. You climb past a wartime lookout by a pyramidal day mark which, as well as aiding navigation, also commemorates the laying of the first transatlantic cable, via Brest to Nova Scotia in 1880. Keep right at a gate and continue between hedges - for long-distance walkers a forgotten experience! Views ahead extend right across to the Lizard at the far end of Mount's Bay.

At a National Trust sign for Treen Cliff, a good farm track leads off

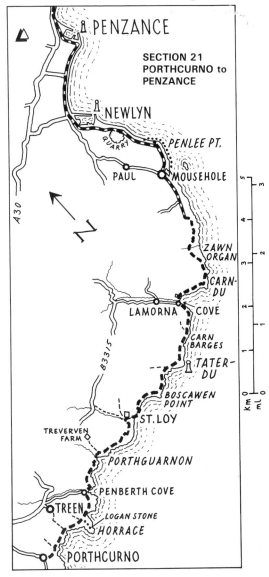

PENZANCE

SECTION 21
PORTHCURNO to
PENZANCE

NEWLYN

QUARRY

PENLEE PT.

PAUL

MOUSEHOLE

A30

N

*ZAWN
ORGAN*

*CARN-
DU*

LAMORNA   COVE

*CARN
BARGES*

*TATER-
DU*

*BOSCAWEN
POINT*

B3315

ST. LOY

TREVERVEN
FARM

PORTHGUARNON

PENBERTH COVE

TREEN

LOGAN STONE

HORRACE

PORTHCURNO

163

left for the village of **TREEN** *(some accommodation, campsite; pub; Post Office/Stores; telephone; car park; toilets)* - about 600m inland and the last amenities until Lamorna Cove, a strenuous 4½ miles (7km) away. You can cut off Horrace promontory by proceeding straight ahead, but most walkers will make the short diversion for a look at the Iron Age earthworks and the famous 'logan' stone atop a chaotic jumble of granite boulders ('logan' means moving or rocking). In fact, 'logan' is a misnomer here, for the stone's original rocking movement was lost after it was dislodged by a party of young seamen from HMS Nimble in April 1824 and subsequently repositioned following a public outcry. The officer responsible for the initial vandalism and for the daunting feat of reinstating the 80-ton rock under orders from the Admiralty, using teams of men and lifting gear was Lt. Goldsmith RN, a nephew of the poet Oliver.

The clifftop path continues over Cribba Head and drops to little **PENBERTH COVE** *(telephone just inland behind a house)* - a huddle of cottages and boats and an interesting old capstan on the slipway. Cross the stone footbridge and walk in front of the cottages. At the top of a rise, keep up left towards a wind vane then turn right at a coast path finger post. The rocky path undulates along above small fields once used widely on this coastline to cultivate daffodils, but now often abandoned.

Getting down and up through Porthguarnon will come as a surprise to those who thought that the real legwork was over and done with! It is a biggish descent to a small waterfall and bouldery beach; beyond the streams a stiff pull up. *(At the top, path left for camping at Treverven Farm.)*

Now on more open, grazed land, bear right past a field gate then turn sharp right at a finger post. Stay down the main path above a patchwork of neat fields and pass a house down to the right. You soon come to a stile (straight ahead to the B3315), where we turn right through an idyllic wood, over a private access track, crossing a stream and emerging onto a beach of large, rounded boulders at **ST. LOY**. This tiny and secluded settlement is reputed to enjoy one of Britain's warmest micro-climates, though baulks of timber and other heavy jetsam also bear witness to the force of storm waves. Great care is needed when boulder-hopping, especially in rain or wind; it is hoped a better path line will eventually be provided, but at present you stay on the beach for about 25m and watch for a path up left by a large rock just past the stream outlet.

More wooded ground follows then you are climbing boggy, rougher slopes to Boscawen Point - efforts are rewarded with excellent views, including ahead to Tater-du lighthouse. The coast path drops right, over a slab and down further before undulating along and climbing to a gate. Go straight on through it and along the lighthouse track to a foghorn warning notice. This fully automated lighthouse was built in 1965 following the loss of 11 crew from the Spanish ship 'Juan Ferrer' - just one of a long series of wrecks on this dangerous coast.

Keep seaward round Carn Barges with its stone monolith. From here to Lamorna Cove, wild flowers and increasingly lush vegetation are a feast for the eyes, though legs and feet will have to deal with very rugged going underfoot. Wild garlic, daffodils, drifts of white narcissi and bushes of starry hawthorn blossom overflow neglected little enclosures from a time when flower growing was profitable.

Reaching a small stone cross down to the right (inscribed 'D.W.W. March 18th 1873', in memory of a Cambridge student who fell to his death), beware the very unstable cliff edge: small yellow arrows act as markers for a 10m detour but it is easy to miss them. Suddenly the path swings north and you are in **LAMORNA COVE** (*cafe; car park; toilets. Inland at* **LAMORNA** - *inn, Post Office/Stores; telephone*).

Above the cove, quarry waste spills down, reminding us that Lamorna once exported high quality granite from its modest harbour, now frequented by scuba divers and holidaymakers. The village is associated with artists (*occasional summer exhibitions*) and with nearby

Lamorna Cove

sites of archaeological interest which include the Bronze Age Merry Maidens Stone Circle (about a mile north-west).

Cross Lamorna Cove's footbridge and follow the path up between cottages. Views soon open out ahead to granite formations on the shapely headland of Carn-du, whose spine is crossed at one of the South West Way's momentous vantage points. Even those who consulted the map beforehand will be taken aback by the great sweep of Mount's Bay from Marazion to Lizard Point. If you are carrying binoculars, the sequence of sandy bay, cliff and settlement can be clearly identified, capped by the distinctive aerial dishes of Goonhilly Earth Station.

The onward path drops right above a rocky foreshore then slants up through dense conifer wood at Zawn Organ. You drop sharp right at a waymark, whereafter the path becomes tortuous and narrow, threading its way above long-overgrown cultivation terraces at Slinke Dean (despite the existence of a true coastline path to seaward, ignored by the authorities). At least there are continuous sea views, before you veer sharply left up old stone steps through derelict walled enclosures to emerge by large rocks and a conspicuous white Coastguard lookout.

At first between hedges, the path widens and reaches the topmost houses of Mousehole. Turn right along the lane and down it, with comprehensive views of town and harbour, leading to the centre of **MOUSEHOLE** - pronounced 'Mowzel' - *(shops and services; accommodation; cafes, restaurants and pubs; Post Office; buses to Penzance; car parks; toilets; early closing Wednesday).*

Exacerbated by the development of better facilities at nearby Newlyn, Mousehole's fishing fleet has suffered a similar fate to that of many other Cornish ports and today the harbour is almost exclusively given over to tourism. Like St. Ives, its population is increasingly elderly, though steep hills and the 'Cornish ailment' - arthritis from the damp air - can hardly add to its attractiveness as a retirement area.

Once a much more prominent place than now, Mousehole was virtually razed to the ground in 1595 by 200 raiding Spanish seamen from France - 7 years after the Armada's defeat - who then turned their attention to Newlyn and Penzance. The little offshore island is named after the patron saint of ships.

Officially the coast path now takes to the coast road round Penlee Point, past the disused Penlee Lifeboat Station which stands as a memorial to the tragedy of 1981 when Mousehole lost 8 of its men who were crewing the lifeboat. The station is now located at Newlyn.

Penlee Quarry and stone-crushing plant can prove irksome in a westerly wind, coating passers-by with dust which, as walkers prepar-

Mousehole

ing to enter the Newlyn/Penzance conurbation you may well resent! A rather more pleasant, if unprepossessing, exit from Mousehole can be made by taking to the ledge of a concrete drain which heads off along the foreshore, seaward of buildings from the eastern end of the harbour car park. There is an hiatus some way along, but the next section can be picked up easily by crossing some rocks; eventually you are forced to walk inland to the road.

NEWLYN spills over into **PENZANCE** *(Between them they possess all the shops, services and places for eating and drinking likely to be needed by coastal walkers (early closing Wednesday). Accommodation is prolific and includes a youth hostel a mile north-west of Penzance town centre at Castle Horneck. Bus services are more plentiful and Penzance is British Rail's main line terminus in the south-west. There are ferry and British Airways helicopter services to the Scilly Isles, 30 miles away.)*

Newlyn's harbour, recently developed, is one of Cornwall's busiest, with a still-flourishing fishing fleet. Dockside buildings house fish freezing and canning plants, while on the South Pier stands the Ordnance Survey Tidal Observatory. Paintings from the Newlyn School of the late 19th century can be seen in the Passmore-Edwards Art Gallery.

There are relatively few really sizeable towns actually on the coast path. Penzance is one and takes its place between Barnstaple and Newquay to the north, and Falmouth, Plymouth, Torquay and

Newlyn Docks

Weymouth to the east. Strategically, Penzance offers an ideal starting or finishing point for long-distance walkers tackling large sections of path, but equally favours the day-walker bent on exploring Land's End, Mount's Bay and the Lizard.

A sea front promenade runs right along from Newlyn to Penzance; to reach it, you pass the fish quay and cross the first small footbridge over the stream, keeping straight ahead to the beginning of the prom with its pleasant leisure gardens. If you are planning to give Penzance a miss (on a winter's Sunday perhaps!), keep walking round past the seawater swimming pool, War Memorial, docks and a vast car park. Soon you reach the railway station and are forced onto the pavement alongside the busy A30 until just before the Heliport.

This is the onward route anyway, but Penzance is worth half a day of anyone's time, whether or not you need accommodation and supplies. Put on the map in the 1850's by the opening of its Great Western Railway station, the town benefitted from increased tourism and more efficient transportation up-country for Cornwall's early vegetables and flowers. This was timely, since mining and fishing would soon decline, leaving less fortunate communities much the poorer.

Even today, any overland journey to south Cornwall seems protracted. High speed trains slow to a sedate pace little faster than their predecessors a century ago as they negotiate Isambard Kingdom Brunel's Saltash Bridge and the tortuous line through Cornwall's green and hilly countryside beyond. Roads are steadily improving but still suffer from chronic congestion during the holiday season.

Distant Penlee Point from Penzance seafront

If you have time for sightseeing, visit the Tourist Information office opposite St. John's Hall, Alverton Street - the main shopping thoroughfare. There you will find details of a town trail, museums, notable buildings, public gardens and a town plan.

NOTES ON TIN AND COPPER MINING IN CORNWALL

Coast path walkers in north Cornwall can hardly fail to miss the evocative ruins of 19th century mine buildings. They occur on clifftops from St. Agnes to Mount's Bay but can also be seen dotting the landscape inland. That all the installations are ruinous tells its own sad tale - only Geevor Mine, north-east of Land's End, continues to extract tin ore commercially and the fluctuating world market ensures a less than certain future for the industry.

It was during the Carboniferous period that molten granite rose into already intensely folded and contorted sedimentary rocks - the so-called Cornish 'killas' - cooling slowly and allowing the formation of its constituent crystals. Collecting specimens of quartz, felspar and mica is still possible well off the beaten track, but many good examples can be seen in museums at Truro, Penzance and Camborne. Under the immense heat and pressure, other liquids and gaseous materials were produced, giving rise to metal ores. Tin and copper have been those principally mined but other such as silver, gold, nickel, cobalt, zinc and iron also exist. The same processes formed china-clay, now extracted mainly in south Cornwall, while another igneous rock - gabbro - is quarried for road stone.

Erosion and movements in the earth's crust over ensuing millenia exposed the ore-bearing granite and once man had discovered how to convert ores into metals, small-scale exploitation began. Indeed, as early as 4000BC, Bronze Age man was trading tin and copper with Ireland and the near continent and it is well known that the Romans used these metals of Cornish origin.

The earliest method of obtaining alluvial tin was 'streaming' - washing the ore from river bed deposits. Mounds and hollows left by prospectors are typical features of the landscape on Bodmin Moor. Later, crude explosives or heating at surface level were used. Mining *per se* would in all probability have begun on coastal cliffs where mineral veins were exposed naturally. 'Adits' - or galleries - were driven in to work the ore-bearing rocks but once tunnelling down became necessary, water posed a real problem.

To pump it out, manpower, horsepower and eventually steam were employed, the latter driving 'man engines' to move miners who previously faced long and arduous descents and ascents on vertical wooden ladders. In contrast to the affluent ease of mine and land owners,

Ruined winding house near St. Just

172

miners themselves led a life of unremitting hardship. Walking to and from the mine head, they worked strenuous shifts below ground in wet and dangerous conditions. Illuminated only by helmet candles, they were sustained by the legendary Cornish pasty, whose thick, crusty ridge was soiled by dirty hands and discarded.

On 20th October 1919 a hinge sheared at the top of the beam engine in Levant Mine (one of the largest mines and situated near Geevor). Instead of transporting miners up and down between platforms in the shaft side - 12ft. (4m) at every stroke - the entire system failed, killing 31 men and seriously injuring many more. It was to prove Cornwall's worst mining disaster.

By the end of World War I, profitable mining in Cornwall was already doomed. From being the world's greatest copper producer after the Industrial Revolution and a major tin producer in the mid-19th century, the industry succumbed to cheaper imports. In 1945 just two mines - Geevor and South Crofty - remained in operation.

Today the acres of spoil are colonised by gorse, heather, brambles and bracken; masonry crumbles beneath the onslaught of wind and rain. Nevertheless, much is revealed to the walker whose unique close-up perspective on the landscape allows for inspection of details and the spanning of history by the use of a little imagination.

In places, the mine ruins have been renovated for safety and posterity - to the benefit of holidaymakers and students of industrial archaeology alike. The surface workings at Geevor are open to the public; elsewhere, ruins are noted in the text wherever the coast path lies in proximity to them. They are most frequent in Chapter 3 between Newquay and Penzance.

DISTANCE TABLE (including major variants.
Approximate mileages rounded up or down.)

SECTION	FROM	TO	ML	KM	ACCUMMULATIVE ML	KM
1	MINEHEAD	Bossington	6	10	6	10
	Bossington	PORLOCK WEIR	3	5	9	14
	PORLOCK WEIR	Wingate Combe	6	10	15	24
	Wingate Combe	LYNMOUTH	5	8	20	32
2	PORLOCK WEIR	County Gate	5	8	Variant	
	County Gate	LYNMOUTH	6	10		
3	LYNMOUTH	Hunter's Inn	5	8	25	40
	Hunter's Inn	Great Hangman	6	10	31	50
	Great Hangman	COMBE MARTIN	2	3	33	53
4	COMBE MARTIN	Ilfracombe	5	8	38	61
	Ilfracombe	Lee Bay	3	5	41	66
	Lee Bay	WOOLACOMBE	4	6	45	72
5	WOOLACOMBE	Croyde	5	8	50	80
	Croyde	Saunton Sands	2	4	52	84
	Saunton Sands	BRAUNTON	7	11	59	95
	Saunton Sands	BRAUNTON via Sandy Lane Farm	5	8	Variant	
6	BRAUNTON	Barnstaple	6	10	65	105
	Barnstaple	Instow	7	11	72	116
	Instow	WESTWARD HO! via ferry	4	6	76	122
	Instow	WESTWARD HO! via Bideford	10	16	Variant	
7	WESTWARD HO!	Buck's Mills	8	13	84	135
	Buck's Mills	CLOVELLY	4	6	88	142
8	CLOVELLY	Hartland Point	8	13	96	154
	Hartland Point	HARTLAND QUAY	3	5	99	159
9	HARTLAND QUAY	Morwenstow	7	11	106	171
	Morwenstow	BUDE	6	10	112	180

SECTION	FROM	TO	ML	KM	ACCUMMULATIVE ML	KM
	BUDE	Widemouth Bay	3	5	115	185
10	Widemouth Bay	Crackington Haven	6	10	121	195
	Crackington Haven	BOSCASTLE	7	11	128	206
	BOSCASTLE	Tintagel	5	8	133	214
11	Tintagel	Trebarwith Strand	2	3	135	217
	Trebarwith Strand	PORT ISAAC	6	10	141	227
	PORT ISAAC	Portquin	2	3	143	230
12	Portquin	Polzeath	5	8	148	238
	Polzeath	PADSTOW via ferry	3	5	151	243
	PADSTOW	Trevone	5	8	156	251
13	Trevone	Trevose Head	3	5	159	256
	Trevose Head	PORTHCOTHAN	4	6	163	262
14	PORTHCOTHAN	Mawgan Porth	4	7	167	269
	Mawgan Porth	NEWQUAY	7	11	174	280
	NEWQUAY	Holywell	6	10	180	290
15	NEWQUAY	Holywell via Trevemper	7	11	Variant	
	Holywell	PERRANPORTH	4	6	184	296
	PERRANPORTH	Trevaunance Cove	3	5	187	301
16	Trevaunance Cove	Porth Towan	4	6	191	307
	Porth Towan	PORTREATH	3	5	194	312
17	PORTREATH	Gwithian	8	13	202	325
	Gwithian	HAYLE	4	6	206	332
18	HAYLE	ST.IVES	7	11	213	341
19	ST.IVES	Zennor	7	11	220	354
	Zennor	PENDEEN WATCH	6	10	226	364
	PENDEEN WATCH	Cape Cornwall	4	6	230	370
20	Cape Cornwall	Land's End	6	10	236	380
	Land's End	PORTHCURNO	5	8	241	388
	PORTHCURNO	Lamorna Cove	5	8	246	396
21	Lamorna Cove	Mousehole	2	3	248	399
	Mousehole	PENZANCE	3	5	251	404

USEFUL ADDRESSES AND TELEPHONE NUMBERS

AIRPORTS:
Bodmin Airport, tel Cardingham (020 882) 463
British International Helicopters, tel. Penzance (0736) 63871
Brymon Airways, tel. Newquay (063 73) 860551
Land's End St. Just Airport, tel. Penzance (0736) 787017
Newquay Airport, tel. Newquay (063 73) 860551
Exeter Airport, tel. Exeter (0392) 67433

BRITISH RAIL PASSENGER INFORMATION:
Penzance (0736) 65831

BRITISH TOURIST AUTHORITY:
Information Centre, 64 St. James' Street, London SW1

BRITISH TRUST FOR CONSERVATION VOLUNTEERS:
36 St. Mary's Street, Wallingford, Oxon. OX10 0EU, tel. (0491) 39766

CAMPING AND CARAVANNING CLUB:
11 Grosvenor Place, London SW1W 0EX

COUNTRYSIDE COMMISSION:
John Dower House, Crescent Place, Cheltenham, Glos. GL50 3RA,
tel.(0242) 521381

EXMOOR NATIONAL PARK AUTHORITY:
Exmoor House, Dulverton, Somerset TA22 9HI

FERRIES:
Instow to Appledore - 'The Seachest', Market Street, Appledore, Devon,
tel. Bideford (023 72) 76191
Rock to Padstow - Black Tor Ferry, Padstow Harbour Commissioner,
Harbour Office, West Quay, Padstow, Cornwall, tel. Padstow (0841) 532239
Newquay to Crantock - Fern Pit Ferry, Riverside Crescent, Newquay,
Cornwall, tel. 873181

FRIENDS OF THE EARTH:
377 City Road, London EC1V 1NA, tel. (01) 837 0731

HOSPITALS (with Casualty Dept.):
Truro City Hospital, tel. (0872) 74242
West Cornwall Hospital, St. Clare Street, Penzance, tel. (0736) 62382

LONG DISTANCE WALKERS ASSOCIATION:
11 Thorn Bank, Onslow Village, Guildford, Surrey, GU2 5PL;
handbook £5.95 post free

NATIONAL TRUST:
36 Queen Anne's Gate, London SW1H 9AS, tel. (01) 222 9251

Regional Information Offices:-
for Somerset - Dorset and Somerset Regional Info. Office, Stourton,
Warminister, Wilts. BA12 6QD, tel. (0747) 840560

for Devon - Devon Information Office, Killerton House, Broadclyst,
  Exeter, Devon EX5 3LE, tel. (0392) 881691
for Cornwall - Cornwall Information Office, The Estate Office,
  Lanhydrock Park, Bodmin, Cornwall, PL30 4DE, tel. (0208) 4281

NATURE CONSERVANCY COUNCIL:
Northminster House, Northminister Road, Peterborough, Cambs. PE1 1UA,
  tel. (0733) 40345
for South West Region - Roughmoor, Bishop's Hull, Taunton, Somerset,
TA1 5AA, tel. (0823) 83211

RAMBLERS ASSOCIATION:
1/5 Wandsworth Road, London SW8 2LJ

ROYAL SOCIETY FOR THE PROTECTION OF BIRDS:
The Lodge, Sandy, Beds. SG19 2DL, tel. (0767) 80551

SOUTH WEST WAY ASSOCIATION:
Membership Secretary, 1 Orchard Drive, Kingskerswell, Newton Abbot,
  Devon TQ12 5DG, tel. (08047) 3061

MAIN TOURIST INFORMATION CENTRES:
Bude - The Castle, tel. Bude (0288) 4240
Padstow - Station House, Station Road, tel. Padstow (0841) 532296
Newquay - Morfa Hall, Cliff Road, tel. Newquay (063 73) 871345
St. Ives - The Guildhall, tel. Penzance (0736) 796297
Penzance - Station Road, tel. Penzance (0736) 62207/62341

WEATHER FORECASTS:
tel. (0898) 500481

WEST COUNTRY TOURIST BOARD:
Trinity Court, 37 Southernhay East, Exeter EX1 1QN, tel. (0392) 76351

WESTERN NATIONAL BUSES:
Tower Street, Taunton, Somerset, or National House, Queen Street, Exeter,
  Devon, EX4 3TF

YOUTH HOSTELS: (in walk order)
Alcombe Combe, Minehead, TA24 6EW, tel. (0643) 2595
Lynbridge, Lynton, EX35 6AZ, tel. (05985) 3237
Ashmour House, 1 Hillsborough Terrace, Ilfracombe, EX34 9NR,
  tel. (0271) 65337
Worlington House, Instow, Bideford, EX39 4LW, tel. (0271) 860394
Elmscott, Hartland, EX39 6ES, tel. (02374) 367
Palace Stables, Boscastle, PL35 0HD, tel. (08405) 287
Dunderhole Point, Tintagel, PL34 0DW, tel. (0840) 770334
Tregonnan, Treyarnon, Padstow, PL28 8JR, tel. (0841) 520322
Alexandra Court, Narrowcliff, Newquay, TR7 2QF, tel. (0637) 876381
Droskyn Point, Perranporth, TR6 0DS, tel. (0872) 573812
Riviere House, 20 Parc-An-Dix Lane, Phillack, Hayle, TR27 5AB
Letcha Vean, St. Just-in-Penwith, Penzance (Land's End), tel. (0736) 788437
Castle Horneck, Alverton, Penzance, tel. (0736) 62666

BIBLIOGRAPHY

Coastline - Britain's Threatened Heritage by Greenpeace (Kingfisher Books)
Cornwall's Structure and Scenery by R.M.Barton (Tor Mark Press)
The Making of the English Landscape by W.G.Hoskins (Pelican)
The AA Book of the Seaside
Cornish Shipwrecks Vol. 2 - The North Coast by C.Carter (Pan Books)
Flowers of the Cornish Coast by J.A.Paton (Tor Mark Press)
Lorna Doone by R.D.Blackmore
South West Way handbook by the SWWA (Devon Books)
Along the South West Way - Minehead to Bude by A.G.Collings (Tabb House)
The West Country Beach Guide by Andrew Carless (Garnet Press)
The National Trust Guide to the Coast by Tony Soper (Webb and Bower)

A COAST PATH CODE

Beware crumbling and unstable cliff edges at all times.

Ensure the tide is favourable before beach-walking beneath cliffs.

If walking alone, leave details of your itinerary with a responsible person.

Keep to the coast path or other definitive rights of way over farmland.

Observe notices and waymarks, especially through M.O.D. property and over private land.

Respect hedges, walls and fences by only crossing them at gates and stiles.

Never pitch a tent on farmland without first obtaining permission to do so.

Avoid damaging plants, trees and growing crops.

Respect the privacy of inhabitants living close to the path.

Keep dogs under close control near livestock.

Take your litter with you.

If you see anyone in difficulties on land or at sea, dial 999 from the nearest telephone and ask for the Coastguard. Being able to give a map grid reference or other accurate positional reference for the incident is of great value to the rescue services.

If you need assistance yourself, the international distress call is 6 long signals (eg. whistle blasts, shouts, torch flashes etc.), repeated at 1-minute intervals. The reply is 3 signals at 1-minute intervals.

A SEA-BATHING CODE

Where possible, bathe within areas patrolled by lifeguards.

Only bathe between the 2 red and yellow flags. Red flags denote danger.

Keep a careful eye on children and non-swimmers - even quite shallow water can be dangerous.

Don't bathe in areas marked by black and white chequered flags - these are for malibu surfboards and canoes only.

Never use inflatables on exposed coastlines and in offshore winds.

Avoid bathing directly after a meal.

Avoid bathing at least one hour each side of low tide or in a heavy swell on unsupervised beaches.

Keep a watchful eye on the state of the tide if bathing beneath high cliffs or in river estuaries.

NOTES

PRINTED BY MARTIN'S OF BERWICK